Stories of Hope and Encouragement to Share

RIPPLES

of

JOY

CHERYL KIRKING

Author and Compiler

SHAW

WATERBROOK

Ripples of Joy
A SHAW BOOK
PUBLISHED BY WATERBROOK PRESS
2375 Telstar Drive, Suite 160
Colorado Springs, CO 80920
A division of Random House, Inc.

All Scripture quotations, unless otherwise indicated, are taken from the *Holy Bible, New International Version*®. NIV® Copyright © 1973, 1978 by the International Bible Society. Used by permission of Zondervan Publishing House. All rights reserved. Scripture quotations marked (KJV) are taken from the *King James Version*. Scripture verses marked (TLB) are taken from *The Living Bible*, copyright ©1971. Used by permission of Tyndale House Publishers, Inc., Wheaton, Illinois 60189. All rights reserved. Scripture quotations marked *The Message* are taken from *The Message*. Copyright © by Eugene H. Peterson 1993, 1994, 1995. Used by permission of NavPress Publishing Group. Scripture quotations marked (RSV) are taken from the Holy Bible, *Revised Standard Version* © 1946, 1952, 1971 by the Division of Christian Education of the National Council of the Churches of Christ in the USA. Used by permission. All rights reserved.

Other permissions and acknowledgments appear on pages 233–238.

ISBN 0-87788-402-1

Library of Congress Cataloging-in-Publication Data
Ripples of joy : stories of hope and encouragement to share / compiled by Cheryl Kirking.
     p. cm.
    ISBN 0-87788-402-1
    1. Christian life—Anecdotes.   2. Anecdotes.   I. Kirking, Cheryl, 1959-

BV4517.R57 2000
242—dc21
                                                                    00-055664

Printed in the United States of America
2000—First Edition

10 9 8 7 6 5 4 3 2 1

To my husband, David Kilker,
for dreaming with me,

and to my children,
Blake, Sarah Jean, and Bryce,
our little dreams-come-true.

Contents

Part Nine: Ripples of Wisdom

Part Ten: Ripples of Laughter

Part Eleven: Ripples of Generosity

Part Twelve: Ripples of Delight

Acknowledgments

Give thanks to him and praise his name.
For the LORD is good and his love endures forever.
—PSALM 100:4-5

A special thank-you to:

Florence Littauer and Marita Littauer, for being shining examples of what it means to speak and write graciously, from the heart,…and to Fred Littauer, too, for your kind encouragement.

Lil Copan and my editors, Joan Guest, Barbara Hicks, and Mary Horner Collins—as well as Laura Barker, Elisa Fryling, and all the good people at Shaw and WaterBrook. I am so grateful.

Jennifer Shipley, for being a sounding board during this project…and a true friend.

my parents, LeVerne and Jean Kirking, and to family and friends for continued support in so many ways.

my children, Bryce, Sarah Jean, and Blake—for lots and lots of hugs and kisses to keep me going.

my husband, David, for sharing "impractical" dreams and practical support—like washing dishes, bookkeeping, and helping me figure out the new computer!

all who submitted stories, each one a splash of inspiration!

you, the reader—thank you. May this book inspire you to encourage others.

Preface

Imagine you are standing by a clear, placid pond. In your hand you hold a smooth, round stone. As you wrap your fingers around it, think of the many things for which you are grateful: your friends, family, health, good food, the beauty of nature. You might be at a place in your life where it's difficult to count your blessings, but you can be thankful for life itself; every breath of life and each beat of your heart is a gift.

Let the stone represent your gratitude. Now imagine tossing it into the pond. Watch the ripples emanate, each ripple creating another.

So it is when we live grateful lives and are willing to share our gifts with others. When we are truly grateful, we can't help but share the blessings we enjoy. We can't keep our joy in! I call it "Thanksliving."

May this book touch your life with splashes of insight and joy and inspire you to encourage others. Let's go make some ripples!

Drop a stone into the water
And in a moment it is gone,
But a hundred ripples circle on and on and on

Say an unkind word to someone
And in a moment it is gone,
But a hundred ripples circle on and on and on

Share a loving deed of kindness
And in a moment it is gone,
But a hundred ripples circle on and on and on...

©1998 Cheryl Kirking/Mill Pond Music

Part One

RIPPLES
of
COMPASSION

Who is thy neighbor? He whom thou
Hast power to aid or bless;
Whose aching heart or burning brow
Thy soothing hand may press.

Thy neighbor? Pass no mourner by;
Perhaps thou canst redeem
A breaking heart from misery;
Go share thy lot with him.

AUTHOR UNKNOWN

The Woman in Seat 10-C

Cheryl Kirking

I made my way to the back of the small commuter plane, a thirty-seat, twin-engine propeller jet. I plunked into seat 10-A, grateful to see there was an empty seat between me and the woman in seat 10-C. I was looking forward to stretching out and relaxing during the hour-and-a-half flight home to Madison from Cincinnati.

I smiled and nodded to the woman in seat 10-C. She appeared to be in her late fifties and had salt-and-pepper hair. She nodded back. As I buckled my seat belt, I felt her looking at me expectantly, as if she wanted to chat, so I asked pleasantly, "Have you heard how the weather is in Wisconsin?"

"No, I haven't," she replied.

"Hope it's not icy," I said. She offered no response.

Maybe I read her wrong, and she doesn't want to talk. Rather glad that I wouldn't have to keep up a conversation, I closed my eyes to rest. Within a few moments, I heard her say something softly.

"Pardon me?" I asked.

"I said you have lovely skin," she repeated.

"Thank you." I smiled. She half smiled and nodded but didn't say any more, so I closed my eyes again.

"You have to take care of skin like yours."

I opened my eyes. "Pardon me?" I wasn't sure I had heard her correctly.

"Skin like yours…you're so fair-skinned. You have to use sunscreen."

"Right. Of course, with the crummy weather we've been having lately, I don't have to worry about the sun these days!" Then I thought, *Why is this lady so interested in my skin? Is this the best she can do to strike up a conversation?*

"Do you have children?" she asked.

Well, at least she's moving on to a topic I enjoy talking about, I thought. "Yes, I do. Three."

"Do they have skin like yours? Fair?"

"Uh, yes they do, pretty fair."

"Do you put sunscreen on them?"

Aha! I'll bet this lady is trying to sell me some kind of skin-care program! I knew she wanted to talk! Not only is she going to try to sell me products, I'll bet she's going to try to talk me into joining a network marketing scheme before we land!

"Yes, I do," I said aloud. "I always use sunscreen. In fact, I have a whole cupboard *full* of sunscreen: waterproof, sensitive skin, you name it, we've got it. We are always ready for any skin-care emergency!" I closed my eyes again, hoping she'd gotten the message that I did not need any skin-care products. Several more minutes passed. I sensed she was looking at me. I opened my eyes and she quickly looked away, her face tense. I noticed her hands clenched in her lap, her knuckles white.

"Excuse me," I asked. "Are you…all right?"

She looked as if she was trying to speak. "I…I…"

"Ma'am?" She seemed ill. "Ma'am, are you feeling okay?"

"I-I'm sorry. I just…I just came from…my daughter's. My daughter just passed away."

I gave a little gasp. I felt ashamed. Here I was thinking the poor woman was trying to sell me something, when what she needed was to talk. "I'm so sorry," I said softly. I didn't know what else to say. After a long pause I asked, "Your daughter…she lived in Cincinnati?"

The woman nodded.

"I'm so sorry," I repeated. "I can't even begin to imagine what you're going through."

She nodded. I wanted to say something of comfort but had no words.

"She and her husband have two children. Boys. They are a blessing."

"I'm sure they are. How old are they?"

"Nine and eleven."

"Do you have any pictures of your grandsons?"

"Yes." She smiled and took out her wallet, which was filled with school photos of the boys.

"They're blond like their mother. Suzanne was fair, like you. She... she died of skin cancer. That's why I hope you...take care of your skin."

I swallowed hard, but my eyes filled and the tears overflowed.

I wiped my eyes and extended my hand. "My name is Cheryl."

She took my hand. "I'm Louise."

We talked for an hour. About the recent months she had spent with her dying daughter. About the unfathomable pain—and the sweet moments of surprising joy. About her grandsons, her family, and her two dogs. About my children. Sometimes we even laughed.

"We'll be arriving in Madison in about ten minutes," the pilot announced.

"I noticed you have a guitar," Louise remarked.

"Yes, I sing a bit."

"What kind of songs do you sing?"

"Mostly songs I write."

"You write your own songs! Would you sing something?"

"Well, I..." I looked around. At least we were in the very last row of seats. Perhaps I wouldn't be heard over the roar of the engines.

"If you don't mind a cappella, I'll sing you the chorus of a song I've been working on."

Drop a stone into the water, and in a moment it is gone,
But a hundred ripples circle on and on and on.
Yes, a hundred ripples circle on and on and on...
A hundred ripples circle on and on and on...

She squeezed my arm. "That was beautiful."

"Thank you," I answered, feeling a little embarrassed.

We would be landing in a few minutes. I was glad that the whine of the engines made it nearly impossible to talk. I looked out the window as we approached the runway. The plane came to a stop, and the lights came on. We got our bags from the overhead bins, chatting about the rain while we waited to get off the plane. As we entered the terminal, I warned Louise to drive carefully in the freezing drizzle.

"My neighbor is coming to pick me up. There she is," Louise said, pointing.

"Well, take care, Louise." I gave her a quick hug.

She nodded. "You know," she said, squeezing my hand. "Your song...the ripples.... Love is like that, isn't it? It goes on and on and on. Love never dies."

I swallowed hard and nodded.

Her neighbor approached us, and we exchanged greetings. As I walked away, I thought about the stone in the water. I thought about Louise's remark, how love never dies. And how every act of love we express can have a ripple effect.

You never know what ripples your words or actions might make in the lives of others.

Offer one small act of kindness and in a moment it is gone
But a hundred ripples circle on and on and on.
A hundred ripples circle on and on and on...

The golden rule of friendship is to listen to others
as you would have them listen to you.
DAVID AUGSBURGER

Tori's Last Chance

Jeannie St. John Taylor

Through all four years of high school, my daughter Tori had faithfully sweated through daily track workouts. Then while the other runners went home to eat dinner, she had sprinted extra intervals with her coach. She did well in races but had never won a district race. And only district winners went to the finals at State…

Tori leaned into her pre-race stretch at the district meet. *This is it— my last high-school race, my last chance to go to State,* she thought. *If I don't win this race, it's over. I have to win this!*

In the next lane, Kate, a senior from a competing school, sprinted up the track and back. She looked tense. They had raced against each other often. Kate had never made it to State either. This was her last chance too.

You're my biggest threat today, Kate. Do you want to win as much as I do?

"Nervous?" Kate asked her.

Tori nodded and jogged in place.

"Races upset my stomach," Kate added.

An official in a black shirt announced, "Ladies, take your places."

"See you at the finish line," Kate said as they positioned themselves in their lanes.

"I'll be there," Tori answered.

"Get set." The official pointed the gun upward.

Lord, help me do my best, Tori prayed. *Let this race bring glory to you. Bang!* The race started.

Tori ran just behind Kate, as Coach had instructed, listening to the sound of Kate's breathing and the pounding of feet on the track. *I'll stick close to her shoulder, then kick it for the final lap,* she thought.

"Perfect pace!" Coach yelled from the sidelines in the second lap.

Tori felt confident, strong. Kate pulled ahead, but it didn't matter. There'd be plenty of time to pass her in the final lap. Tori relaxed into her stride, one foot in front of the other in a steady rhythm.

By the time Tori finished the second lap, the pack of runners had already fallen half a track behind. *No need to worry about them. I'll just glide behind Kate, then pass her when Coach gives the signal.*

Near the end of the third lap, Coach signaled for Tori to move up.

Here I come, Kate. She strode out, closing the distance between them. Kate must have sensed it. She glanced back at Tori, red-faced and worried.

You're tired, aren't you? Tori thought. She pumped her arms and legs, pulling up beside Kate.

The two girls ran side by side now, their breathing nearly drowning out the roar of the crowd. The bell sounded as they rounded the turn into the final lap. Two more steps and Tori surged past her, glancing sideways at Kate's face as she passed. Kate looked pale and sick—the way Tori had felt her freshman year when she'd collapsed at the finish line.

She's done! I'm going to win!

Then somehow, out of nowhere, Kate was beside her again on the outside, passing her. Kate's breathing sounded in rasping gasps. She exhaled in grunts.

"No!" screamed Coach. "Don't let her pass you! Push harder!"

Tori willed her legs to move faster, but they wouldn't. As though seeing in slow motion, she watched Kate move two, then three strides ahead of her. Then, almost at the finish line, Kate suddenly pitched forward and fell facedown on the track, unconscious, her body pushed to exhaustion.

I won!

For a split second Tori exulted in her victory. Then she stopped cold, her feet inches from the finish line. *No. I won't win this way. Kate gave all she had. She deserves first place. I'll drag her over the line before I cross it.*

Tori ran back and grabbed Kate's legs. Slippery with sweat, they slid from her hands and fell limply onto the track. Tori could see the pack of runners bearing down on them. She grasped Kate under the arms and pulled. As she yanked her over the line, she felt the whoosh! whoosh! whoosh! of three other runners crossing the finish line.

Did I pull Kate across in time?

Kate's eyes fluttered open and a teammate hurried over to help her to her feet. Tori paced with her hands on her hips, getting her breathing under control. Had Kate won?

She found out soon enough, when an official handed her opponent the first-place marker. Tori smiled at Kate, but disappointment lumped in her throat and she fought tears. *I'm not sorry. But I did want to compete at State.*

At that moment another official held out the second-place marker to Tori. "Congratulations," he said. "You're going to State."

"What?" Tori asked, confused.

"The back of your foot crossed the finish line before the other runners. First- and second-place winners compete at State," he said. "Didn't you know?"

"No, I didn't."

Tori smiled again. *You are so good, God!*

In a race everyone runs, but only one person gets first prize. So run your race to win. To win the contest you must deny yourselves many things that would keep you from doing your best. An athlete goes to all this trouble just to win a blue ribbon or a silver cup, but we do it for a heavenly reward that never disappears.

1 CORINTHIANS 9:24-25, TLB

Dave's Goofy Day

Carmen Leal

The day, our only day to go to Disney World, is picture perfect.

An answer to prayer for my husband, Dave.

Dave loves Goofy. In fact, what Dave feels for Goofy borders on obsession. For Christmas I gave him his heart's desire, two Goofy shirts, which he wears almost exclusively.

It's no surprise that the last thing on Dave's to-do list is going to Disney World.

Dave is dying. He is in the last stages of Huntington's disease, a rare, devastating, degenerative brain disorder for which, right now, there is no cure. At forty-six years of age, Dave shuffles through his days like an old man of eighty. As his appetite and ability to swallow continue to decrease, so does his weight.

Sometimes I am not sure who lives in his body: the three-year-old child or the old man who sits and stares into space. On this day there is no question. It is the three-year-old, dressed in his purple Goofy shirt, eager and excited.

I could never afford Disney tickets for my family of four, but I want to give Dave a special day; I know time is running out. Thanks to the generosity of the wonderful Disney Compassion Program, today we are going to make a memory.

As excited as Dave is about the excursion, I have a nagging concern. What if we get to the park and Goofy can't be found?

No need to worry! Look! There's Goofy, right inside the front gate, holding court with dozens of young fans clutching their autograph books, faces glowing as they wait to greet their favorite character. I wheel Dave's chair up the ramp and wait behind the children, none of them older than five. I alternate between feeling happy for Dave and feeling unbearably sad for myself at the loss of my dreams. Before Huntington's disease ravaged his brain, Dave had earned a master's degree in business administration. Now the crowning achievement of his life is getting to spend time with Goofy.

It's Dave's turn. His smile is ecstatic. Goofy seems to know he's special. Dave gets extra time for hugs, a caress on the arm with the floppy ear, a kiss on the cheek. A lady in line offers to take a Polaroid picture for Dave so he has an immediate keepsake of the event rather than having to wait for our film to be developed.

I am trying hard to smile, but it's difficult to breathe as I watch Dave's childlike delight through a veil of tears.

We buy a colorful Goofy doll, which Dave keeps safe in the shopping bag. Every few minutes, though, Goofy comes out of the bag. Dave talks to him and beams.

In his wheelchair, Dave gets the royal treatment; there are no lines for us as we breeze through the park. Dave and Goofy enjoy every ride, even the scary ones. It is truly a perfect day.

Tonight Dave sleeps with Goofy, and whenever the doll gets tangled in the covers or falls to the floor, he wakes me to find it. I know that when the hospice workers come tomorrow, he will trip over his words as he relates the story of his day with Goofy.

In the morning Dave tells me that now, since he got to meet Goofy, God can call him home so he can see the angels in heaven. But I think Dave has already seen some angels. I'm convinced that Donna with the Disney Compassion Program and the employee in the Goofy suit are angels. Only an angel would have treated Dave with such dignity and joy on his extraordinary day. And the caring lady, conveniently standing nearby with a Polaroid camera, just has to reside in heaven.

Part of me is happy to give Dave his Goofy day. Another part mourns for the husband I thought I had already said good-bye to years ago. I feel a loss as I have not felt since he was first diagnosed. Sometimes I wonder how I can ever survive, but I know God will continue to bring angels alongside me whenever I really need them.

He always does.

What do we live for, if it is not to make life less difficult for each other?

GEORGE ELIOT

Rose-Colored Glasses

Liz Hoyt

Looking back, I suppose I should have seen it coming. But Beth Ann is a sweet, loving soul. I never suspected she would outsmart me.

I had Beth Ann's best interests at heart. She was always involved in some self-sacrificing service project or another, and I was determined to rescue her from her life of drudgery. I'd convinced her to spend a fun day with me, shopping, visiting, and enjoying lunch. I let her select the day for our outing, the Sunday before Thanksgiving. Perfect for me: I was expecting twelve guests for Thanksgiving, and my lavish dinner plans demanded new table decorations. Spending a day in the city was just what I needed before the hectic holiday season got underway.

Life in the Texas hill country is pretty relaxed, so I didn't think it unusual when Beth Ann suggested we wear jeans and sweatshirts for our shopping spree. Besides, my favorite home-decorating boutique didn't care what I wore as long as I remembered to bring my credit cards.

The Texas sky was clear on the morning of our outing. The Christmas decorations in my little town sparkled in the morning sun, and I hummed "Jingle Bells" as I turned onto the highway for the short drive to Beth Ann's house on the outskirts of San Antonio. Beth Ann is a quiet, gentle spirit with a quick laugh and mischievous, twinkling eyes. She views everyone with a heart of love, and spending time with her always warms me. But that day I was on a mission! Under my expert guidance, Beth Ann would "see the light." She'd finally update her closet and cosmetics. She'd learn to spend more time on herself. After all, she wasn't getting any younger.

She was waiting when I pulled into her drive. We hugged, and she sweetly urged that we continue in her car. I hate riding in her old rattletrap; she hauls just anybody and anything in it, and it smells like it! My luxury sedan, on the other hand, is comfortable and smells of scented apples.

But you don't argue with a dear soul like Beth Ann, so we were quickly on our way in her smelly and noisy vehicle, laughing, talking, and catching up. I told her about my Thanksgiving plans, my grandson's latest achievements and awards, and the expensive Christmas gifts I planned to buy for my grown children. I entertained her with stories of my busy life in a small town, and in between, in spite of the bumpy ride, I wrote out lists of all the things I needed to purchase that day.

When Beth Ann stopped the car, I absently looked up from my shopping list to see that she had parked among other cars and pickups under a major interstate highway—in what appeared to be an inner-city, asphalt parking lot that sprawled as far as I could see. People of all colors, sizes, and ages were unloading old, beat-up serving tables, card tables, ice chests, and huge coffee urns. They were apparently turning the dirty parking lot into a giant, outdoor dining room.

"Beth Ann, darling—where are we, and *what* are we *doing* here?!"

She smiled at me with the tender expression of an angel, handed me a bundle, and said, "Put on this apron, my precious friend. It is time you gave up your rose-colored glasses!"

With that she jumped out of the car, laughed, and put the keys into the pocket of her jeans. I had to run to catch up with her, and we were immediately caught up in the mass of dirty, smelly remnants of humanity milling around, waiting expectantly. The noise from the busy highway far above mingled with the banging and clanging of pots and pans on the dismal parking lot.

Beth Ann waved to one and then another of those filthy beings, calling out greetings and addressing them by name. Leftover dregs of society came up to her to smile and say hello. She talked to each of them. She even—God forbid—*hugged* them!

Then she quietly ordered me to help the people who were setting up the serving area and unloading huge pans of turkey, dressing, sweet potatoes, collard greens, and pumpkin pies. I was furious. My "friend" had tricked me into serving Thanksgiving dinner to bums and losers who wandered homeless and lost on the city streets.

When the food was spread out, the crowd organized itself into orderly lines without fanfare, instruction, or greediness. My hands trembled with disgust and anger as I began to fill plate after plate. The line was endless, and the faceless mass of humanity kept coming.

I don't know when things changed, but slowly I began to see individual faces. Eyes filled with weariness and pain. One by one the hungry filed by. Some stared straight ahead, their eyes blank; some smiled shyly with heads down; some thanked me; many looked at me and said, "God bless you, lady."

Faces became names. Minutes melted into hours, and the names became real people who were afraid, lonely, and hungry. By the time the food was gone, my fear, disgust, and anger had drained away into exhaustion. A sweetness I had not felt in years poured over me, and I found myself smiling, listening, and yes, even touching.

Beth Ann and I never got to the boutique that day. My mission to rescue and change her was forgotten; instead, I was the one who was changed. I had looked into the faces of weary, hurting people and allowed myself to reach into their hungry souls. I took off my rose-colored glasses and left them lying on that dirty parking lot where real people had shared time, food, and Thanksgiving hope with each other.

"Someone ought to do it, but why should I?"
"Someone ought to do it, so why not I?"
Between these two sentences lie whole
centuries of moral evolution.

ANNIE BESANT

The Quiet One

from the life of Kim McDaniel
as written by her sister, Kaye D. Proctor

The girls on the tenth floor were a rowdy bunch. We worked the afternoon shift at the bank, from 3:00 P.M. until midnight. All the checks bank customers had written during the day passed through our processing machines during those evening hours. It was my job to supervise the little crew and make sure, through all the horseplay and rough girl talk, that work actually got done. Most of the time I was able to balance being the good-old-girl and trying to keep the lid on things so the work was done correctly.

Jan was hired about a year after I started my supervisory job. She was a very frail-looking girl with light red hair and pale blue eyes, and she was extremely quiet. Her first night on the job she asked me if she could use the bathroom. I told her she didn't need permission.

I noticed the "Previous Experience" section of her job application was sparse. One of my big complaints about my job was that, although I supervised, someone else did the hiring. *Here we go again,* I thought. *This shrinking violet will never fit in here. They've given me a problem.*

During the first month Jan was absent three days, and I decided to have a chat with her. She looked crestfallen when I called her into my cubicle. She explained to me in hushed and halting tones that she had been diabetic since early childhood, and health was sometimes an issue. She apologized for her absences and swore she could promise better attendance in the future. I was skeptical, but she looked so sincere that I couldn't doubt she meant to keep her promise.

I noticed the other girls gave Jan a wide berth, pretty much ignoring her, even at lunchtime when they were all busy talking about boys and hair and clothes and movies. Jan, at age twenty-two, still lived at home and didn't have much of a social life. Her mom dropped her off at work, and her dad picked her up. She never contributed to the conversations except to offer to help clean up the lunchroom or to help out another girl who had gotten behind in her work.

Wanting to encourage her, I offered her tips on how to win the monthly employee contest. When I could, I ate lunch with her. She told me about her luck growing plants and invited me over to her house to see her sunroom, crowded with exotic specimens she had successfully nurtured. One Monday she brought some pictures of an orchid that had bloomed over the weekend. I regret to say that, with my busy life, I never saw the actual flower.

One Friday night about six months after Jan started, we heard shouting down the hallway. *Fire!*

I ran to take a look. A corner of our paper supply room had burst into flames. I called 911, and the fire department responded right away. The brisk blaze was contained successfully, but not before we had evacuated the tenth floor. With almost two hours lost, our productivity had suffered. I asked for volunteers to work late, but most of the girls had reasons they couldn't help me out. Only Jan quietly said she would be glad to stay.

We worked together until almost 4 A.M. to finish up. She chatted cheerfully about her family and pets. By this time she was comfortable with me and was opening up a lot more. She even talked about a young man at church that she had her eye on. I remember being a bit overtired and telling silly jokes to pass the time. She giggled happily. I noticed she looked pale, but my focus was on getting the work done and getting home. "Thanks so much for staying," I told her when we were finished. "See ya Monday."

But I didn't. I never saw her alive again.

Jan's mom called Monday afternoon to tell me that Jan had passed away the morning after we worked together. Her diabetes had taken its final toll on her heart. She had gone to sleep and never awakened.

I was stunned. It had never occurred to me that she was that delicate. She was so young that her death seemed impossible. I forgot to ask her mother about funeral arrangements, but her sister called a few hours later and gave me the information, asking if I could attend. I said I would.

I felt very odd the morning of the funeral. I hadn't really known Jan very well and thought I would feel awkward at the service. But I had accepted the invitation and was determined to see it through.

Jan's father greeted me with a warm smile and handshake at the door of the church. "You're Kim, aren't you?"

"Yes, I am. I'm so sorry about your loss."

He nodded. "We are so pleased that Jan's best friend could be here today," he said. "She spoke about you often and told us you were the closest friend she had ever had. Thank you so much for what you meant to my daughter."

The words had barely sunk in when Jan's sisters and mother surrounded me and voiced the same sentiment. They gave me a place of honor at the front of the church, reserved for those closest to the deceased, and I was the guest of honor at the little reception at the family home after the funeral. I had been important to Jan, and now I was important to her family as well.

Whenever I question whether I truly can have an impact on others, I remember Jan. I'm grateful I was able to make a little room for her in my busy life back then. Yes, I wish I had done more. But Jan taught me that it's never too late: Opportunities for small kindnesses surround me every day.

Next time, I'll be sure to go see the orchid.

There is not a person we employ who does not, like ourselves, desire recognition, praise, gentleness, forbearance, patience.

HENRY WARD BEECHER

Part Two

RIPPLES
of
LOVE

Love is always building up.
It puts some line of beauty on everything it touches.
It gives new hope to discouraged ones, new strength
to those who are weak.
It helps the despairing to rise and start again.
It makes life seem more worthwhile to everyone
into whose eyes it looks.
Its words are benedictions.
Its every breath is full of inspiration.
AUTHOR UNKNOWN

The Little Red Boots

Jeannie S. Williams

When my granddaughter, Tate, celebrated her fifth birthday recently, her mother gave her a very special present: a pair of red cowgirl boots that had belonged to her when she was a little girl. As Tate slipped on the little red boots, she began to dance across the room in excitement.

My mind flashed back to the afternoon my daughter-in-law, Kelly, showed me the little red boots and told me about the first day she had worn them. You see, not only had Kelly experienced the thrill of wearing her first pair of real cowgirl boots back then, but she had also experienced the thrill of meeting her first love.

He was her first "older man"—she was five and he was seven! He lived in the city, and his father had brought him to Kelly's grandfather's farm one Saturday afternoon to ride the horses. Kelly sat on the top fence rail, watching her grandfather saddle her pony. She was proud of her shiny new red boots and was trying hard not to get them dirty. Just then the city boy came over. He smiled at Kelly and admired her boots. It must have been love at first sight because Kelly found herself offering to let him ride her pony. She had never let anyone ride her pony before.

Kelly's grandfather sold the horse farm later that year, and she never saw the little boy again. But for some reason she never forgot that magical moment when she was five, and every time she put on her red cowgirl boots she thought of the cute city boy. When Kelly outgrew the boots, her mother decided not to throw them out, but to pack them away. After all, Kelly had loved the little red boots so much.

Many years passed. Kelly grew up into a beautiful young woman and met my son, Marty. They married and had their daughter. One day while Kelly was rummaging through some old boxes in preparation for a garage sale, she found the little red boots. Fond memories flooded into her heart. *I used to love these boots,* she recalled with a smile. *I think I'll give them to Tate for her birthday.*

Tate's laughter brought me back to the present, and I watched as my son scooped his giggling daughter up in his arms and danced around the room, her red birthday boots on her feet. "I sure like your new cowgirl boots, baby," he told her. "In fact, for some reason they remind me of the day I rode my very first pony. I wasn't much older than you."

"Is this a true story, Daddy? Or a make-believe one? Does it have a happy ending? I like stories with happy endings," Tate said. She loved to hear her daddy tell stories about his childhood and begged him to tell her about his first pony ride. Marty laughed at Tate's never-ending questions and sat down in the big recliner as Tate climbed onto his lap.

"Once upon a time," he began, "when I was seven years old, I lived in the big city of St. Louis, Missouri. And do you know what I wanted more than anything in the world? A horse! I told my dad that when I grew up I wanted to be a real cowboy. That summer my dad took me to a farm not very far from here and let me ride a real pony. I remember that there was a little girl on that farm, sitting on a fence, and she was wearing new red cowgirl boots just like yours."

Kelly sat listening to Marty telling their daughter about his first pony ride. When he got to the part about the red boots, her eyes grew wide in amazement, and her heart filled with wonder: Marty had been the cute city boy she'd met back when she was only five years old!

"Marty," she said, her voice trembling, "I was that little girl. That was my grandfather's farm. And those are the same red boots!"

Tate sat happily in her daddy's lap, unaware that in that magical moment her parents realized that they had met as children, and that even back then they had felt the special connection between their hearts.

Where there is great love, there are always miracles.
WILLA CATHER

Learning Love
from a Labrador

Vivian Gall

My recovery from an intricate foot surgery was long and difficult, and I was feeling very sorry for myself, confined as I was to a wheelchair or hopping about balanced on a walker. I despaired of ever walking again and enjoying normal mobility. To make matters worse, it was summer, and I missed being near the soothing seaside and watching the waves roll in.

One weekend, my daughter Cindy, her roommate Georgan, and their two handsome Labradors came to visit. They had driven from central California in a van large enough to accommodate all of us, including my wheelchair. When asked where I'd like to go for a drive, I immediately responded, "To the beach!"

"Dog's Beach" is a special section of the coastline nearby where, for a stretch of a mile, dog owners are allowed to run their dogs. Naturally this is where we went, especially as the dogs had never experienced the ocean and the girls were eager to see their reaction.

My wheelchair could not manage the sand, so the girls set me on the sidewalk high above the water, where I had a good view and could watch them play fetch with the dogs. It was fun to see the girls toss a stick into the waves and see the dogs happily bark as they retrieved the sticks and brought them back for more of the game.

Their play had gone on for about ten minutes when one of the dogs, Sky, suddenly left the water's edge and ran up the bank of sand to the sidewalk where I was sitting. She came up to me, laid her head on my lap, and gazed into my face with her beautiful eyes as if to say, "Are you all right? I know something must be wrong if you're not down by the water with us." I gave her a big hug and encouraged her to go back to play.

A few minutes later, Sky was back again, checking on me, head on my lap, and telling me with her eyes, "I care about you." Those eyes of hers, those soulful eyes, brought me close to tears.

When we got home and the dogs and girls were hosed off and fed, I was relaxing in an armchair with my cast-enclosed foot up on an ottoman. Soon Sky was at my chair, her head in my lap and her eyes telling me that she was still on duty watching out for me. So expressive were her eyes that I could almost hear her words of concern and support.

When the visit was over and the girls had gone back to central California, the memory of Sky stayed with me. She had taught me a lesson: Just the expression of caring and concern had a salutary effect. It made me feel warm and secure—and yes, loved.

Time passed. I healed and went back to my work as a school librarian.

Back at work, I used the lesson I had learned from Sky to change how I dealt with staff and students. Where once I had passed another teacher with just a quick "Hi," I now slowed down, made eye contact, asked "How's it going today?" and waited for an answer. When students seemed overwhelmed by all the books to choose from, I took time to ask about their interests and guided them to books they might like.

Taking the time and extra effort to show caring and support was more than its own reward. The staff now comes into the library with big smiles, and the kids think it's a good idea to give me a hug as a thank-you for the experience of a book they enjoyed.

I hope this will be a permanent way of life for me—showing that

I care. After all, what would Sky think if I failed to put into practice all she's taught me?

He who does not live in some degree for others,
hardly lives for himself.

MICHEL DE MONTAIGNE

Circle of Love

Jeannie S. Williams

When Joey was five years old, his kindergarten teacher told the class to draw a picture of something they loved. Joey drew a picture of his family, and then he took his red crayon and drew a big circle around the stick figures on his paper. Joey wanted to write a word at the top of the circle, so he got up from his chair and approached the teacher's desk.

"Teacher," he asked, "how do you spell—?"

But before he could finish his question, the teacher told him to go back to his seat and not interrupt the class again. Joey folded the paper and stuck it in his pocket.

When Joey got home from school that day, he remembered his drawing and dug it out of his pocket. He smoothed it out on the kitchen table, got a pencil from his backpack, and looked at the big red circle. Joey's mother was busy cooking supper, but Joey wanted to finish the picture before he showed it to her.

"Mom, how do you spell—?"

"Joey, can't you see I'm busy right now? Why don't you go outside and play? And don't slam the door," she told him.

Joey folded the drawing and stuck it back in his pocket. Later that evening Joey dug the picture out of his pocket again. He looked at the big red circle and then ran into the kitchen to get a pencil. He wanted to finish his drawing before he showed it to his father. Joey smoothed out all the wrinkles and laid the picture on the floor near his dad's big recliner.

"Daddy, how do you spell—"

"Joey, I'm reading the paper right now, and I don't want to be bothered. Why don't you go outside and play? And don't slam the door."

Joey folded the drawing and put it in his pocket. His mom found the drawing the next morning while she was doing the laundry. She threw it in the trash without ever opening it, along with a small rock, a piece of string, and two marbles Joey had found while he was outside playing.

When Joe was twenty-eight years old, his daughter Annie drew a picture. It was a picture of their family. Joe laughed when five-year-old Annie pointed to a squiggle stick figure and said, "That's you, Daddy!"

Annie laughed too. Joe looked at the big red circle his daughter had drawn around the stick figures and began to slowly trace the circle with his finger.

"I'll be right back," Annie said as she jumped off her father's lap. When she came back she had a pencil clutched in her small hand. Her father moved the drawing aside to make room on his lap for his small daughter.

Annie positioned the pencil point near the top of the big red circle. "Daddy, how do you spell love?" she asked.

Joe gathered the child in his arms and guided her small hand as he helped her form the letters.

"Love is spelled T-I-M-E," he told her.

We need to think of the home as the cradle into which the future is born, and the family as the nursery in which the new social order is being reared. The family is a covenant with posterity.
SIDNEY GOLDSTEIN

My Father

Tom Suriano

When my brother and I were boys, every morning as far back as I can remember my father came into our bedroom bright and early, turned on the overhead light, pulled the covers off our beds, and said in a very loud and distinctive voice, "You still in bed? Half the day is gone!" It was 7:00 A.M. But if you slept after that, you were just plain lazy, and he wouldn't hear of that—not his sons!

My father worked thirty years in a factory and never missed a day of work until he was diagnosed with cancer and forced to retire. He was a jack-of-all-trades: carpenter, electrician, plumber, mechanic, bricklayer—there was nothing he couldn't do. And he never made a mistake; he would just say, "That's the way I wanted it!"

My father's dream was to build his own home for his family, but we were always just a little too poor. And our "new" car was always someone else's, though it was new to us. Dad and Mom bought and paid for two homes and always had food on the table, clothes for our backs, and the cleanest house in town. They also put my brother and me through college and graduate school. But my father never got to build his own home, as he had always dreamed of doing.

When I was thirty-five years old and the father of two daughters, my wife and I decided to build our own home. This was going to be a true milestone in our family's history! I was a college graduate with a master's degree, and now I was building my own home. It didn't get any better than that for an Italian family who "came over on the boat" in the early 1900s.

My wife and I finalized blueprints for our house and hired a con-tractor. I'll never forget the day I went to my father's home to share the news. I was so proud that I thought I would burst. And I believed my dad would be just as proud and happy for me.

He wasn't.

Now sixty-five years old, my father had just beaten cancer for the second time. He looked up at me from the kitchen table and said, "Boy, I strongly think you shouldn't do this."

Talk about taking the wind out of my sails! This *wasn't* the way it was supposed to go. I was going to build the home he had always wanted to build, and he should have been excited for me.

I just stood there, stunned, and asked him why. Dad said very emphatically, "You don't have enough money or skill to build a house, and I'm too old now." Of course I disagreed and said I was going to do it anyway, with or without his blessing. Big talk from a guy who couldn't even drive a nail.

I didn't have enough experience, he said. Besides, building a house was only half the job; there were a million things I hadn't even considered. It would take us ten years to completely finish the home we wanted to build. And on and on. My mother, on the other hand, told us to do what we wanted and wished us good luck.

We began by getting a loan from the bank and lining up all the contractors and subcontractors. It didn't take long for me to have to eat crow. I came up $3,000 short for securing the loan, and we hadn't even started. With hat in hand, I went to the "old man" and very humbly asked if I could borrow $3,000. I assured my father I would pay him back on his terms any way he wanted it.

Dad was sitting at the kitchen table with my mother, having a cup of coffee. He said to my mother, who is the financier of the family, "Write the boy a check for $5,000." I thought he misunderstood me, so I repeated myself. He said he had heard me, and that I was the one who didn't understand. Dad said he had already anticipated I'd come up short, and he and my mother had decided to give me $5,000 as a gift to get us started.

Tears were now flowing down my face. I saw an old man who had never missed a day's work in thirty years giving his hard-earned money away to a son with big ideas and little money to back them up. My mother just got out the checkbook and wrote me a check as my father had requested.

But our problems had just begun. The contractor started building in February. My wife and I are both schoolteachers, and neither of us could be there in the daytime to supervise the job. So I did what I always did: I went and got the "old man" and told him to run the show! Now he got tears in his eyes, and I had my own foreman— good for me, bad for all the contractors and workers. If it wasn't perfect, he would make them start over and do it again. He was their worst nightmare, and when they threatened to quit, I just reminded them who was writing the checks and that the "old man" was calling the shots, period. Everyone began to work hard, fast—and politely— until the last check was written.

But my problems still weren't over. One day the money was gone and so were the workers—and my house was only three-fourths finished. The night after the last worker left, I went to bed in my new and unfinished home. The children had been in bed for hours, and my wife had fallen asleep earlier from exhaustion. I was lying awake, staring at the ceiling and thinking, *What in the world am I going to do now? No money and no skill!* I didn't sleep all night.

At 7:00 A.M. sharp the next day, I heard a car coming down the gravel road of my dead-end street and saw headlights shining through my bedroom window. I jumped out of bed like a little kid on Christmas morning, ran down three flights of steps with my pajama bottoms on and threw open the basement door. There was my dad, bigger than life, with his ball cap on, and all the tools, shovels, and picks he could fit into his brand-new car—and it finally was his *own* new car. As I stood there barefoot in my pajama bottoms, he just looked at me and said, "Hey, boy, you still in bed? Half the day is gone, and we've got a lot of work to do!"

With a lump in my throat and tears in my eyes, I just stood there, speechless. I was never so glad or so relieved to see the "old man." Now I knew everything was going to be okay. And why shouldn't it be? Dad had always been there when I needed him.

Five years later, my new home is completely finished inside and out, all three floors plus the landscaping. For all those five years, my dad never missed a day's work at my house. The "old man" is the most hardheaded, hard-nosed, and loving man I've ever met. I hope he lives forever, but if he doesn't, I know where to find him. He'll be fixing the golden gates in heaven.

One father is more than a hundred schoolmasters.
GEORGE HERBERT

Love Extravagantly

Marita Littauer

"Have a mission statement!"

That's what I encourage readers to do in my book *You've Got What It Takes!*

Then I looked at my own life. I realized that I had a defining statement or theme for my professional ventures, but I did not have a personal mission statement. I knew how valuable my professional statements were, so I could easily see the importance of having a personal one. Here I was recommending something to my readers I hadn't done for myself.

I mulled the idea over in my mind for several days, focusing on the need for a personal purpose statement, the "path" I wanted for my personal life.

At that time I was attending a women's Bible study on the book of Ephesians. As a part of my personal preparation for the study, I was reading the Bible passage covered each week in several different versions of the Bible. I wasn't looking for a personal mission statement, although it had been in the back of my mind. I was simply preparing for the lesson. But as I read from Ephesians one night, a verse jumped out at me and I instantly knew it was my personal "path"—at least for then: "Observe how Christ loved us. His love was not cautious but extravagant. He didn't love in order to get something from us but to give everything of himself to us. Love like that" (Ephesians 5:2, *The Message*).

As I read that verse, I knew my personal mission: to love my husband, Chuck, with extravagance—not to *get* but to *give of myself.* As I cook breakfast or dinner, as I do the dishes, as I do the laundry—all of these things are something of myself I can give, not expecting to get in return. I have written the verse out and placed it on my mirror in the bathroom to remind me that loving extravagantly is my mission. I find that I have to repeat the mantra to myself frequently, as it is contrary to my human nature.

Shortly after taking on this idea of loving extravagantly, I had to put it to the test. Chuck has a large, radio-controlled model airplane that has been a part of his life for over twenty years. He built it and has too much of himself invested in it to risk flying it. With a five-foot wingspan, it doesn't fit just anyplace. In our current home it hangs up near the peak of the cathedral ceiling in the family room. It is bright red with Red Baron–like decals. It is sure to be noticed. Since it is important to my husband, I have accepted it as a conversation piece—and you can be sure it is! It has traveled with us to eight different houses.

Recently Chuck took the airplane down to take it to a model airplane show. He spent hours cleaning off the accumulated dust that had firmly attached itself to every surface. The plane was very popular at the show, and he discovered how valuable it really is. Before he put it back on its hook, he wanted to protect it—so he covered the body and wings with plastic dry cleaning bags. Advertising and all!

I like my home to look like a showplace. You can imagine that even having the airplane hanging from the ceiling is an act of compromise and love. But having it covered with baggy dry cleaning bags went too far. "I'll never be able to entertain again," I wailed.

After my outburst, which I knew was an overreaction, I went outside to trim my roses. As I took a deep breath, "love extravagantly" came to mind. *Does it really matter if the airplane has a bag over it?* I asked myself. *What is more important: that my husband be happy or that I have a lovely home?* Hmm—that was tough!

"Love extravagantly," I told myself. I came back in and apologized—ready to accept the dry cleaning bags. Meanwhile he had decided that I was right and it was really ugly. He had taken the plane down, removed the dry cleaning bags, and was replacing them with clear plastic wrap that clings tightly to every curve and doesn't even show!

Ah, the power of a personal mission statement! To make my love not cautious but extravagant, to have as my purpose not to get, but to give. What changes do *you* need to make in order to love *your* spouse that way?

> *Keep thy eyes wide open before marriage; and half shut afterward.*
>
> THOMAS FULLER

Through the Eyes of Love

Annie Chapman

I had spoken at a ladies luncheon. As I was packing up, a gentleman who was on staff at the church came to ask me for a favor. He explained that his wife had looked forward to the luncheon and had planned on coming that day, but because of her health, she was unable to attend. He asked if I would mind stopping by his house on the way out of town to say hello to her. I agreed.

As we entered the front door, he told me a little of their story. They had married about fifteen years earlier. I looked at their wedding pictures as he told me of their first year together. She was strikingly beautiful, tall and slender, with long chestnut brown hair. They were indeed a handsome couple.

Life had gone on as expected, he said, until one day she fell down. The falls became more frequent; she realized she was losing strength in her legs. A trip to the doctor sadly revealed a fast-growing form of multiple sclerosis. This terrible disease viciously attacked her nervous system, leaving her in a wheelchair.

Even having heard the story, I was unprepared when I met her. We entered the bedroom, and there she lay, her body twisted and deformed, bearing no resemblance to the beauty queen in the wedding pictures. Gone were the long, flowing locks of brown hair. Instead she wore a manageable, short, cropped style more suitable for the years she had spent in bed.

I glanced up at the husband, and what I saw nearly made me blush. I was standing in the presence of two people very obviously in love. The way this man looked at his wife, the way she teasingly flirted with him, was so personal and deeply intimate. I felt honored, yet somewhat intrusive, to have shared that moment.

As I stood there in the room, I realized why their interchange seemed so special: Without question, I was observing true love. The kind of love that has no conditions. He loved her not for what she could give him—obviously she was more than limited in her ability to express her love—but he loved her because she belonged to him.

This couple had found what the whole world is looking for. While the rest of this crazy, sexually frustrated, morally perverse society is bounding from one encounter to another, true love is found in the privilege of belonging.

In the eyes of the world, this poor, disfigured woman could have been seen as one who had nothing to contribute to her family or society—but through the eyes of love, her husband saw a woman of tremendous value.

And so did I.

Love is a great beautifier.

LOUISA MAY ALCOTT

The First Birthday Party

Kathleen Ruckman

I blew up balloons, hung crepe-paper streamers across our kitchen doorway, and wondered, "Is this worth all the effort? She won't remember anyway."

We had given Elnora, my husband's mother, a birthday party every year, but still she would say, "No one has ever given me a birthday party."

Alzheimer's disease had crept in and robbed Elnora not only of her ability to remember her own birthdays but also of the certainty that we loved her. She would often say, "I never see you," even though we saw her twice a week.

I struggled to accept Elnora's forgetfulness. This was difficult for me, especially in the beginning when we weren't sure yet of the diagnosis. I asked God to give me more patience and understanding.

God answered my prayer by bringing inspiration from a most unexpected source—Elnora herself.

In earlier days Elnora and I had often exchanged prayer requests. However, once the Alzheimer's disease worsened, I had quit asking her to pray. Then my mother was diagnosed with cancer. I will never forget the day I asked Elnora to pray over the phone with me for my mother. Among our many telephone prayers, I particularly remember that one: Her prayer made sense, and her words flowed without her usual confusion, expressing genuine compassion and sadness.

My mother lived to have two more summer visits with us in Oregon. After I returned from her funeral, I once again asked Elnora, who had continued to decline from her disease, to pray. As we sat at my kitchen table, she took my hands in hers and prayed that God would be with me and with the rest of my faraway family.

Like a child, I "peeked" during her prayer. Her eyes squinted shut, she prayed from her heart. That's what I remember most—the earnest expression of one who had loved my mother and who loved the Lord. Her words were beautifully said, almost eloquent. Tears in her eyes lingered after her prayer.

But soon confusion returned. Within a couple of moments Elnora had forgotten my mother had died.

How could this be? In some wonderful way, I believe, the spirit and mind must be separate—and Elnora must still know God. Even when she no longer recognized her family, she recognized her Lord. She communicated with him in her heart—even when she could no longer talk to us. Even in the later stages of her disease, nurses and aides often saw her at the end of a difficult day kneeling and praying at her bedside, her hands folded.

I hung a few more party streamers, deep in thought. I placed the heart-shaped cake I had baked on the center of my kitchen table. Even though her mind wouldn't hold the memory, surely her spirit would grasp the love we would give her. I hung a sign that read, "Happy Birthday, Mom. We love you."

Not worth the effort? A birthday party that Elnora would think of—at least for a little while—as her very first? This party would be very special. And I could hardly wait!

Nobody has ever measured, not even poets, how much the heart can hold.

ZELDA FITZGERALD

My Job

Carmen Leal

I am a caregiver. My forty-seven-year-old husband, David, has a little-known genetic disease called Huntington's disease. He can do almost nothing for himself.

I can tell you that caregivers experience a wide range of emotions, depending largely upon the person for whom we are caring. Lately, I have to admit, I've been feeling there's really no reward for what I am doing.

David has difficulty feeding himself, and swallowing is accomplished only with a great deal of effort. One day, with more food landing on his shirt than in his mouth, David and I were going through the usual "change the shirt" game.

"David, lift up your arms," I pleaded. And then, "If you do, we can go and have ice cream."

David's garbled speech made his response to my urging impossible to comprehend. I did figure out, however, that he had no intention of lifting his arms or cooperating as I changed his shirt.

I felt myself tense up, and I sighed in frustration. I didn't need this today. Try as I would, I simply couldn't understand what he was saying. And we weren't moving any nearer our goal—getting him into a clean shirt.

"David," I finally said, "my job is to feed you, make sure you take your medications, and help your doctors and nurses. Your job is to help me help you. You need to lift your arms, please."

With an endearing smile so like that of the man I had married before the ravages of Huntington's disease took him away, David said, "No. My job is to say 'I love you' in as clear a voice as possible."

Caregiving is not something I would ever choose to do. I imagine most people would not choose what is usually an almost thankless job—especially without pay. Still, there are rewards. Remembering David's smile and his comment about his "job" is a nice memory I can pull out on days when things get really tough. We all have our jobs, and David's job is to say, "I love you."

David, I love you too.

Riches take wings, comforts vanish, but love stays with us. Love is God.

LEW WALLACE

Part Three

RIPPLES
of
PRAYER

*Practical prayer is harder on the soles of your shoes
than on the knees of your trousers.*
AUSTIN O'MALLEY

The Peacekeeper

Gloria Cassity Stargel

The day our younger son, Rick, left home for the Marine Corps was a heart-wrenching one for me. Besides the fact that I just hate good-byes, this was my "baby" going off to become a fighting man. I couldn't help worrying that military training would destroy Rick's loving, compassionate spirit. *Dear Lord, make him tough, if necessary. But, please, Lord,* I prayed, *keep him tender.*

Now, who but a mother would make a request like that?

Rick endured the rigors of basic training and officer candidate school. Then, after advanced instruction, he was assigned to the Marine Corps air station in Cherry Point, North Carolina. There—seeking a little off-duty peace and quiet of his own—he rented a small house out in the country. Always athletic, he looked forward to the solitude of his daily six-mile run along picturesque fields and meadows.

A problem developed, though. It seems that each farm had several large dogs who didn't take kindly to this strange intruder racing through their territories. Every day, by the time Rick made it back to his house, he was tripping over a whole pack of yelping dogs, most of them snarling at his heels. His daily runs were not the tranquil times he had envisioned.

Hoping to discourage the attackers, he tried kicking, swinging a stick, yelling. Nothing worked. Then one day, Rick phoned home. "Mother," he began, "you know those dogs that have been making my life miserable? Well, I remembered you taught us 'kindness always pays.' So I decided to give it a try."

"What did you do?" I asked.

"Yesterday as I ran," he said, "when my patience had been pushed to the limit, I just stopped in my tracks, whirled around to face them, stooped down on one knee, and talked to them in my best 'pet-talk' voice. And you know what?" Rick's voice was smiling now. "Those dogs started wagging their tails and kissing me on the face, each trying to get closer than the other."

"What happened today when you ran?" I wanted to know.

"You wouldn't believe the difference," Rick said. "It was so peaceful! Passing one farm after the other, the whole crowd fell in and ran as usual. But this time they ran with me—not against me. I must have looked like the Pied Piper by the time we got back to my house."

I smiled into the phone, picturing my young, still-sensitive son. Rick had solved his problem.

And God had answered a mother's prayer.

An ounce of mother is worth a pound of clergy.
SPANISH PROVERB

He Said, "I Love You"

Florence Littauer

My friends Jan and Don Frank, believing that children grow up reflecting what they have seen their parents do, have used much of their family time over the years to instill Christian principles in their daughters' hearts.

Wanting to train their children to hear God's voice, when the girls were still young, Jan and Don instituted a new method of prayer for the family. On the first occasion, they all sat on the floor and prayed that God would speak to each one of them. After a period of silence, Don closed their quiet time in prayer. When he looked up and noticed tears in little Heather's eyes, he asked her what was wrong.

"You didn't give God enough time to talk to me," the six-year-old lamented.

At bedtime Jan sat down with Heather on the side of her bed and prayed again that God would speak to her. They waited quietly, and after a while Heather lifted her head with a smile.

"Did God speak to you?" Jan asked.

"Yes," Heather said softly.

"What did he say?"

"He said, 'I love you.'"

What a beautiful lesson for all of us! As we make prayer a part of our everyday lives, we show our children that conversation with God is a normal function and not a boring religious ritual. We teach them that when we are his, we can hear his voice.

> *Let the children come to me, do not hinder them;*
> *for to such belongs the kingdom of God.*
>
> MARK 10:14, RSV

Pennies from Heaven

William Schlegl

Eleanor and I started our married life thirty-nine years ago as under-paid parochial schoolteachers. We didn't make much salary, but our enthusiasm was high.

From the outset of our marriage, we agreed that I would handle the finances and bill-paying chores. Both our paychecks would go into the same account, from which we'd pay our bills. I made sure the Lord's offering was always paid first, and he made sure there was always enough money for our family's needs.

After twelve years of teaching in parochial schools, I decided to apply for a job in the public-school system. I knew that religion was off-limits in public schools, but I felt I could still serve the Lord in my new position, if only in small ways.

Over the years, although our family never acquired what you would call wealth, we always had food on the table and managed to pay our bills. When college time came, our son, Bill Jr., needed a car. I made a deal with him that I would pay his insurance premiums if he would handle all the other expenses related to his car.

One evening, as I was at my desk doing the bills, Eleanor came into the room to announce that supper was ready. She couldn't help noticing my frown. "What's wrong, Bill?" she asked.

Reluctant to answer, I finally replied meekly, "I can't pay all the bills this month. Billy's car insurance—$252—put me over the limit. I don't know what to do."

Eleanor looked over all the papers and bills and checks and envelopes scattered across my desk. Then she noticed a check sitting off by itself. "What's that?" she asked.

"Our church contribution," I replied.

She looked at me happily and said, "Bill, you've always paid our offering to God first, and you still do. He won't forget you. He's taken care of us all these years, and He's not about to stop now. Something will happen to help you pay Billy's insurance."

I tried to smile and say something positive, but all I could muster was a wan, "Let's eat."

The next day, back in the classroom, I was still distracted by the thought of Billy's bill. I needed a miracle.

As I was diagramming something on the chalkboard, the assistant principal walked into the room. This was not unusual, for he makes a point of visiting the classrooms regularly. The students and I just went about our business.

On this occasion, though, the assistant principal didn't stay to observe the lesson. Instead, he walked over to my desk, placed an envelope on my plan book, smiled, waved, and walked out.

My curiosity soon got the best of me, so I gave the students some quiet work to do and sat at my desk. I opened the envelope. To my utter disbelief and delight, inside was a check from the school district, payable to me, for—believe it or not—$252.

It seems that, as a result of the last teacher contract, certain faculty—including me—had accidentally been overlooked for our special raise. The assistant superintendent had discovered the mistake and asked the school board to correct this error. As things turned out, the amount owed me was $252, precisely the amount I needed for Billy's bill!

Some would say this was pure coincidence. Eleanor and I would say it was the Lord answering our prayers. Whatever you give to him, he gives it all back many, many times over, in one form or another.

We know not what the future holds, but we know who holds the future.

WILLIS J. RAY

Promises Kept

M. Patton

Events that would forever change the lives of two young brothers started when John was twelve and Malcolm was eleven. At the time they were visiting their grandmother's farm in Goodlettsville, Tennessee. Though the boys were supposed to go to church that morning, they had decided to go crow hunting instead, so they stayed home with their aunt and uncle.

As the boys prepared to go hunting, they loaded the rifle, set it in a corner of the living room, and filled their canteens. Because they weren't allowed to go after crows until their aunt and uncle left for church, the boys got to feeling their oats and started roughhousing. Before long Malcolm, who had forgotten that the gun was loaded, picked it up and began pointing it around the room. John shouted, "Don't point that thing at me—it's loaded!"

"No, it's not," Malcolm said as he squeezed the trigger.

But it was. The rifle went off, and a bullet hit John in the side of the head. The saving grace was that he had on earmuffs fitted with a thin steel band that clamped the muffs to his head. That metal band split the .22 cartridge into several pieces so the bullet didn't go as deep as it would have if it had been whole. Yet the fragments crushed the entire side of John's skull and went into the brain.

Seconds after the shot rang out, John hit the floor yelling, "You shot me!" He fell with his head next to the bed, so all that could be seen was blood trickling onto the rug. Malcolm thought for sure that his brother was going to die. Their aunt heard the shot and came running. She knelt down, took a close look at John, got up, and ran out into the yard, where her husband was preparing to go to church. They put John into their car and took him over to the funeral home for transfer to an ambulance. From the funeral home, the boys' aunt and uncle went with the ambulance to the hospital. All this time, Malcolm was left alone at the house. That was the first time he had ever prayed in earnest.

"Dear Lord," he pleaded, "let my brother live. Let him live, and I'll become a preacher." Up until that moment, he had never even thought of being a preacher!

On the way to the hospital, John began praying in earnest also. Over and over again, as he felt the blood oozing from his head, he said, "Dear Lord, let me live, and I'll become a doctor."

When John got to St. Thomas Hospital, the brain surgeon told his parents, who had arrived by that time, that the damage was severe enough that while the boy might live, he would probably be a vegetable—unable to walk or talk or do anything for himself for the rest of his life.

When Malcolm got to the hospital later on, he was told the same awful news about his brother. Overcome with remorse, Malcolm was left alone in a small room with only his thoughts for company. That was when the Lord spoke to him—the first and last time he ever had an experience like it in his life. God clearly told him, *John is going to be all right. Don't worry about it.*

It wasn't long at all before John got strong enough to go back home—but he still couldn't talk. By then it was summer. The house didn't have air conditioning, so the windows were kept open most of the time. One afternoon, the family was sitting in the kitchen, not far from John's room, when all of a sudden they heard someone going, "Ugh, ugh." They rushed into the bedroom and discovered that a wasp had gotten under John's blanket. It was then that John decided he would talk.

Doc McClure thought John's recovery was such a miracle that he got doctors from all over the area to come and look at the boy and check his x-rays to confirm it.

Did the boys keep their promises to God?

While Malcolm did become a preacher, the fact is he tried everything he could to get out of it. After high school, he attended Martin College. He was sitting in his dormitory room one Friday evening when the district superintendent walked in and said, "Someone told me you want to be a preacher; is that right?"

Now Malcolm didn't remember telling anybody he wanted to be a preacher—in fact, he was certain he hadn't breathed a word to anyone! "Yeah...yeah, I guess that would be nice," was his less than enthusiastic response.

"Well, that's great, because we got a little circuit down here in Wayne County, Tennessee, that doesn't have a preacher. They will be looking for you this Sunday."

As it turned out, those Wayne County folks may not have wanted a preacher. But then, Malcolm was the nearest thing to nothing they could have found. So they sent him to the largest circuit in the state, where he started pastoring six churches. In 1957, Malcolm got his license to preach, later attended Vanderbilt Seminary, and has enjoyed pastoring ever since.

Now what about John, his brother? He not only recovered, he became an all-around athlete. He played football, basketball, track, and more. He graduated as valedictorian of his high-school class with the highest grade-point average in Marshall County, Tennessee. After that, John entered Sewanee University, where he finished his premed studies in three years. He later became a board-certified radiologist and went on to achieve the rank of colonel in the U.S. Air Force. Today, John is a partner of the Rush Medical Clinic in Meridian, Mississippi.

Now you may be wondering how I've come to know so much

about these two boys. That's not hard to explain. I'm Malcolm. Rev. Malcolm Patton. And John—Dr. John Patton—is my brother.

Prayer requires more of the heart than of the tongue.

ADAM CLARKE

Did You Say "Ham Hock"?!

Glenda Barbre

"That will be $3.00," the butcher informed me, his face smiling over the glass counter.

"You're kidding! $3.00 for this tiny ham hock?"

He shrugged his shoulders in agreement. "I know, prices are high."

My voice nonchalantly replied, "That's okay, I won't take it."

In a practiced manner, the butcher put the ham hock back in the meat case. "I understand," he said kindly.

Carrying my groceries to the car, I prayed silently: *Lord, please help us! You know how hard it is to work the hours I do. You know my husband is injured, and I have to watch every cent. Please, Lord, bring these prices down!*

Seven miles later, pulling in the driveway, my worries hadn't lifted. I fumbled with my keys, juggling the grocery sacks, and then glanced at a paper bag that someone had left by my front door while I was shopping. After I set the groceries in the kitchen, I went back outside and opened the bag. I reached in and found a bundle wrapped in the familiar white butcher paper. *What in the world?* I wondered, and then looked at the stamped ink: HAM HOCK.

I opened the butcher paper. I was stunned. It really was a ham hock. Three times bigger than the one I couldn't afford! *The butcher couldn't have brought this here,* I thought. *He doesn't even know me.*

Deciding to get to the bottom of the mystery, I started calling every friend I knew. After the third phone call, Terry said, "Yes, I put the ham hock on your porch. I was putting meat in my freezer, and deep in my heart and spirit I felt that I was to take you a ham hock. In fact, I heard these words in my soul: *Take Glenda a ham hock.*

"I couldn't get a thing done until I got in the car and took you a ham hock. I know it's really weird, isn't it? I mean, I've never given people ham hocks for a gift. I even said 'Lord, did I hear you say "ham hock"?' It's not my usual gift, you know!"

I then told Terry about the incident in the market and how I had prayed for relief from high prices and wept on the way home because of anxiety over finances. Terry rejoiced with me as she realized she had functioned in the Spirit, obeying God's will beyond logic, appointed to be his delivery system. My heart broke into praise: *God, I am in your care. You do know my needs. Thank you!*

Soon after, a large ham hock simmered with beans on the kitchen stove. The delicious scent filled the air—along with my gratitude.

> *The test of thankfulness is not what you have to be thankful for, but whether anyone else has reason to be thankful you are here.*
>
> AUTHOR UNKNOWN

Dear God...

Cheryl Kirking

He stumbled on the little train
Left out on the floor again,
The one he'd told his son to put away;
He'd have to have a "talking to,"
And as he headed for his son's room,
He stopped to hear his little boy say:

"Dear God,
Please tell my Mommy that I love her
And that we wish she'd never gone away.
Daddy says that she's your special angel
And that we'll meet in heaven someday!
And, God,
Could you ask my Mommy if she'd help you
Choose another mommy for our home?
Though we're doing fine, I think that it is time
We had another mommy for our own."

She locked the door, turned out the light,
Another day, another night,
Another year had come and gone.
She missed the child she'd never had
And the man who would have been a dad,
And she holds on to a faith that's nearly gone.

She prayed,
"God, please tell my darling that I love him
And that I wish he'd never gone away;
I know that he's your special angel
And that we'll meet in heaven someday.
And, God,
You know I want to live my life by your plan,
And if you will, I'll live my life alone…
Though I'm doing fine,
I wonder—is it time
For me to have a husband of my own?"

He stumbled on the little train
Left out on the floor again,
The one they'd told their son to put away;
Taking his wife by the hand,
He said, "Let's go talk to him,"
And as they neared his room they heard him say:

"Dear God,
Thank you for the baby that you gave us!
She smiled when I gave her the new toy;
Mom says she's glad you sent a sister
'Cause she already has a little boy.
And, God,
Please tell my first Mommy that I love her
And that I think about her every day;
Mom and Daddy say that she's your angel
And we'll all meet in heaven someday!"

When all else is lost, the future still remains.

C. M. BOVEE

Part Four

RIPPLES

of

FORGIVENESS

*Only the brave know how to forgive;
it is the most refined and generous pitch of virtue
that human nature can arrive at.*

LAURENCE STERNE

The Broken Angel

Ellen Seibert Poole

Crash!

The sounds of glass shattering mixed with two little girls' sounds of regret echoed from the upstairs bedroom. I bounded up the stairs and discovered a pile of fractured ceramic birthday angels and the dismounted shelf that had formerly displayed them. The figurines belonged to my nine-year-old daughter, Andrea, who was not home at the time.

Andrea's angel collection consisted of nine delicately painted ceramic angels of graduated sizes, bearing numbers from one to nine. Each had been a gift from her grandparents on the corresponding birthday. This treasured collection now lay in pieces on the dresser and floor—and my seven-year-old daughter, Erika, and her neighbor-friend, Jessie, hovered nearby with their best "I'm innocent" expressions.

Knowing that rambunctious Erika and her equally energetic friend were capable of great mischief, I demanded, "What happened?" Receiving only sketchy information, I became suspicious and began to interrogate. Details remained fuzzy, but I got the picture that Jessie had somehow bumped the display shelf as part of a climbing-jumping maneuver involving the top bunk bed. This had caused the shelf to fall off the wall and the figurines to tumble.

When Andrea returned home that afternoon, I gently told her of the accident with her angels. Surprisingly, her first words were, "Is Jessie all right? Did she hurt herself?"

My heart was pierced. What a picture of compassion and forgiveness from a nine-year-old! I felt a mixture of admiration for my daughter and shame for my own harsh, detective attitude.

Using large amounts of Super glue and a week's worth of evenings, my dear husband painstakingly reassembled the pieces of Andrea's angels. Most of them nearly achieved their former appearance. But Angel number five had many visible cracks and chips—even a few gaps where the pieces were too badly smashed to be glueable. Although Jessie's mother offered to replace Angel number five, I declined. The broken angel had taken on new significance as a visible reminder of the beautiful character qualities developing in Andrea.

Years later, when the grandparents generously presented a replacement for Angel number five, I still could not bear to discard the original. It had become a monument. Andrea's birthday-angel collection, now complete from one to sixteen, officially has two Angels number five. One is perfect; the other is precious.

You have hidden these things from the wise and
learned, and revealed them to little children.
MATTHEW 11:25

Liberation Day

Beverly Harding-Mullins

As an American soldier during World War II, H. C. Kiser Jr. was shot down while on a mission over Nazi Germany and captured. He spent seven months as a prisoner of war. Time and time again he experienced God's grace and miraculous intervention as he suffered the hardships of battle and imprisonment. But for the nineteen-year-old Virginia farm boy, the greatest miracle was yet to come.

H. C. grabbed for the bread that the German soldier dangled in front of him. Again "Jim" jerked it back, and this time threw it to his well-fed German police dog. The dog gobbled it down greedily.

H. C. was dying. He now weighed only eighty-six pounds, and his flesh hung on his protruding six-foot-two-inch frame. His body was ravaged from hunger and the physical abuse of walking through war-torn Germany in the freezing temperatures and rough terrain—with little rest. He was walking the one-hundred-mile "Death March" from Nuremberg to Moosburg.

As if the physical abuse were not enough, the German guard whom H. C. had named Jim seemed to delight in destroying the spirits of the young American soldiers. H. C. had become the chief recipient of Jim's cruel taunting.

The Death March was rightly named. The young POWs endured torture by the German guards, the harsh elements, and even, to their horror, inadvertent bombing by their own American planes. Not knowing that the thousands of men marching in columns were POWs, thinking they were enemy troops, American P-47 Thunderbolts and P-51 Mustangs would fly over each day at noon and bomb and strafe their own with machine gun fire.

With bodies of American soldiers flying through the air from the force of the bombing, the desperate POWs were saved only by their own ingenuity. Gathering anything white—clothing, paper, whatever they could find—they spelled out AAF (Army Air Force) and POW (Prisoner of War). H. C. scrambled to help in the mission, but though he ripped pages from an agricultural book, he was not willing to tear pages from his Bible—his only source of nourishment, his Bread of Life. This time, when the American fighters flew over as usual at noon, they banked up and flew on.

The men were starving. The only food the U.S. POWs had was what they could steal or find along the road, and that wasn't much; it was March, and there was nothing to steal out of the fields. Sometimes, if they were fortunate, they would stay at a barn and steal potatoes or grain, which they ate raw—mixed with rat droppings. Anything to sustain life. Most nights they slept without shelter, with no relief from the bitterly cold nights of Germany.

One night the prisoners had bedded down in a huge forest. It was still March, and it began to rain. The rain turned to sleet, and the sleet turned to ice. H. C. had an overcoat he had taken from one of his friends who had died, and he used it for a blanket. The next morning when he woke up, the overcoat was frozen stiff with ice. The guards told the prisoners to get up and get moving. H. C. took the overcoat, frozen into a sheet of ice, and leaned it against a tree before he started to walk. He had lost all feeling in his body; his feet were frostbitten. He looked back and could see slender mounds with a thin layer of ice over them. He begged to be allowed to try to move the mounds—the bodies of men, his friends—to see if any of them were still alive. But Jim prodded him roughly with his gun and said, *"Nein, raus!"* "No, keep moving!" Meanwhile hundreds of young men lay frozen to death or dying.

H. C.'s feet were completely frozen. He had gone for weeks without removing his boots because he knew he would be unable to get them back on. He had no control of his bowels or bladder, and he was running a high fever. He was crawling by now, digging into the earth to pull himself up a hill, and all he could think was, "Please, Lord, don't let me suffer this hell and then be killed."

Jim walked up to H. C. and reached into his overcoat, taking out a piece of bread. He sliced it and held it out to H. C. Still on the ground, H. C. reached up for it, and Jim jerked it back. He held the bread out to H. C. time and again, jerking it back each time H. C. would reach for it. Jim then reached into his other overcoat pocket and took out a block of cheese. Using his knife, he sliced off a piece and held it out to H. C., taunting him. Again H. C. reached up for it. He was so hungry and so desperate. Jim laughed and stuck it in his own mouth, then threw the next bite to his dog. By this time H. C. had gathered enough strength to curse Jim and lunge at him. Jim shouted and the huge police dog charged toward H. C., knocking him back to the ground. H. C. shouted in a raspy voice, weak with hunger and parched from thirst, "I hate you! I will kill you!"

Several days later, walking through a small town in Germany, H. C. spotted leaves of cabbage lying on the ground. They were bleached out from the sun and shriveled. H. C. was feeling delirious. He started over the garden fence after the cabbage leaves. Jim put a shell into his gun and screamed, *"Halt, nicht ruhren!"* "Halt, don't move!" He took aim. H. C. began to rant and rave, "Fellas, Jim is going to shoot me. He is going to shoot me for going over here and getting rotten cabbage leaves." H. C. looked Jim in the eyes, cursed him, and challenged him to shoot. Jim hated H. C., and H. C. hated him even more.

The fifteen thousand prisoners reached their destination, the final prison camp, Stalag VIIA in Moosburg. About six weeks went by. Then, on April 29, 1945, the Fourteenth Armored Division of Patton's Third Army burst through the big iron gates of the prison. The POWs heard the clanging and cleats of the big American tanks as they roared out of the grass and into the camp. Many of the American troops who had come into the camp began to cry as they saw their fellow soldiers. They were filled with rage at how their comrades had been treated.

The Fourteenth Armored Division forced the German soldiers to throw their guns and ammunition down and march into a large building. Then the American soldiers lined up the German guards around the perimeter wall, where they set up a kangaroo court, letting the prisoners be judge. If a guard had been good to a prisoner, the prisoner could spare the guard's life by simply saying so. But if any had harassed prisoners, maimed them, or deprived them of food, he was singled out and killed.

H. C. could hear sporadic gunfire and knew that several ruthless guards were being shot. As he watched the guards being led at gunpoint over a ridge about fifty feet from the building, he began to recall the time of his capture, remembering the feel of a gun and bayonet against his back. He knew his life had been spared.

The American prisoners were lined up and were going around to each of their guards, making the decision whether to let them live or have them killed. It was a terrible decision to make. H. C. shook hands with some of the guards who had been kind to him, and he wished them Godspeed. Then he came to Jim. They were both about the same height, and they were literally face to face. Jim was still in good physical shape. H. C. had entered the army weighing 176 pounds. Now weighing 86 pounds, he stood before Jim, his tormentor, and said, "Now you are the POW, and I am the free man." Jim would not make eye contact with him and became short of breath, knowing that at this moment H. C. could have him killed.

Perspiration began to soak through Jim's uniform. H. C. bowed his head and prayed, "Lord, help me make a decision here. Should I have this man killed? You know what he did. What should I do?"

Waiting, he heard the Spirit speaking to his heart: *H. C., you know when you were dead and trespassing in sin, I shed my blood on Cal-*

vary's cross, and I forgave your sin. Why don't you forgive him like I forgave you?

H. C. thought for a moment, then whispered, "Thank you, Jesus." He reached out and shook Jim's hand. An incredulous smile slowly spread across Jim's face. They couldn't speak each other's language, but H. C. communicated the love and forgiveness that comes from Jesus—a love that crosses all communication barriers and transcends emotions. H. C. was liberated from his captors that day, but he experienced a greater freedom in that holy moment—the freedom of forgiveness.

> *But I say unto you, Love your enemies, bless them that curse you, do good to them that hate you, and pray for them which despitefully use you, and persecute you; That ye may be the children of your Father which is in heaven.*
>
> MATTHEW 5:44-45 (KJV)

Triumph over Evil

M. C. Burns

It was one of those days so gray there doesn't seem to be a horizon. It suited our destination. At the Breendonck camp in Belgium, used by the Nazis in World War II, everything seemed unforgiving.

Our guide took us past the wall against which prisoners had been shot and into the cement-floored room where other prisoners had been tortured. A chain by which people had been hoisted for beatings hung from the ceiling.

We walked through the dormitory rooms, packed with bunks too narrow and too shallow for comfort. We ran our fingers across the graffiti carved in the wooden beams, names of people who, perhaps, had never left—who had only their names to leave behind.

At the end of the tour, our guide told us he had been a prisoner at Breendonck during the war. He had dedicated his life to telling his own story and that of the camp. "People must never forget what happened here," he said. He had been fortunate. In spite of starvation and torture, he'd emerged from the camp alive. He was able to find his sweetheart, who had also been imprisoned.

They married and had two children. Their son was born severely mentally handicapped. Their daughter was born without a hip. The doctors said their children's birth defects were caused by the harsh treatment the man and his wife had received at the hands of the Nazis.

Yet standing there, leaning on the handle of his now-grown daughter's wheelchair with tears in his eyes, he said, "I cannot hate those people for what they have done to me and to my family. For as soon as I begin to hate, I become just like them."

I will permit no man to narrow and degrade my soul by making me hate him.

BOOKER T. WASHINGTON

Because We Love

Laura Kaiser

I was fourteen years old when my mother died after a long and difficult battle with breast cancer. She left behind three children and my dad, who was devastated by her death. We were a close family, but it was my father who really mourned her, the love of his life. He sank into a deep depression, unable to eat or function within even the most normal of parameters.

This began in 1977, when "depression" was defined as "sick in the head." We did not talk about it among ourselves—the anger, misery, and hopelessness that Dad's depression brought to the entire household. I don't think that any of our friends or relatives even guessed how desperate Dad felt. He was able to maintain his work schedule but would sleep every other waking hour. He left for work when we kids (we were fourteen, thirteen, and twelve) were still asleep ourselves, and he returned to bed as soon as he got home, about 2:30 in the afternoon. We simply did not see him. And we were glad to miss him—he was so miserable himself that he didn't care how he treated others. We grew to shy away from him, hoping to avoid his displeasure, his explosion of temper. Often he would threaten to send us to foster homes if we were not more "cooperative" or better at cleaning the house or whatever reason he happened to choose at the time.

We learned to cook, each of us trying different recipes to give the others a break; my specialties were baked chicken and tuna salad. My brother learned to make meat loaf. Going to the grocery store with Dad was another ordeal. He would inevitably make a scene in the store if the checkout line was moving too slowly or if the boxboy did not place the canned goods in a bag separate from the eggs. Many times he stormed out of the store, yelling and leaving the cart, full of food, at the checkout counter. Through it all, we three kids grew closer, keeping the pain to ourselves. Somehow we coped.

Two years went by, and Dad eventually came out of his depression. He joined a group for widows and widowers that met at the local hospital and began to enjoy life again. He took up square dancing, lost weight, and even began to date a little. (Later my sister and I would laugh about those days—we girls were forbidden to telephone boys, but when Dad began to circulate again, widows from his club began to phone him almost daily!)

By the time I graduated from high school, four years after Mom died, Dad was back to his old self: kind, generous, and deeply committed to his children. A few months before I was to leave for college, he wrote me this letter:

My Darling Laura,

This should be a happy time, but it saddens me. You are no longer a little girl that I, in my odd way, can dote over. You are now a lovely, intelligent, personable young lady who will soon no longer be with us. It grieves me that I won't see or speak to you each day.

I'd like to protect and shelter you from life's hardships and disappointments for as long as I live. But I cannot live your life nor would you allow it. You'll manage well without my butting in. As long as I live, I'll be there—but you'll have to ask for counsel.

My treatment of you, particularly during and after the time Mom died, was often harsh and unfair—and that bothers me very much. Please forgive me for this and for the many, many mistakes I've made.

It's very important to me that you know that I love

and treasure you. I marvel each day that God was so kind as to entrust you to me. You've given me so much joy and direction in an otherwise pointless life.

My beautiful daughter—I wish you happiness and contentment all the days of your life.

I love you,

Dad

My father died three short years later, of complications from diabetes and high blood pressure. He was fifty-nine. Even now, twenty years later, this letter brings tears to my eyes.

People ask me how I was able to get through those days after Mom died, when things were so chaotic at home. "Didn't you resent your dad?" they ask. "How did you ever forgive him?"

Now when I look back on those days, I don't recall feelings of resentment or bitterness. I think the reason was expressed in my dad's letter. Before Mom died, our home was blanketed with love and affection—not spoken perhaps, but felt nonetheless. Even when Dad was at his worst, I never felt that we had been completely abandoned, just that we were undergoing a period of difficulty. I knew that we would eventually reach the other side—scarred, maybe, but intact. I knew that my father loved me, even when he was too far away to express it.

Do we always need to forgive our loved ones for their mistakes? It seems to me that life is a series of forgivings, continual and unconscious. This is the true expression of love, that we let go of the things that others do to us. Forgiveness is not something we do publicly for the approval of others but privately, from within. Because we love, we forgive.

Could a greater miracle take place than for us to look through another's eyes for an instant?
HENRY DAVID THOREAU

Seeds of Forgiveness

Norwegian Folk Tale

A man's child was killed by a neighbor's dog. Revenge would not long satisfy this man, so he found a better way to relieve the agony of his heart. That year a famine had plagued the people, and the neighbor's fields lay bare—he had no corn to plant for next year's harvest. So the grieving father one night sowed the neighbor's field. His reason? "I sowed seed in my enemy's field that God might exist."

Whatever a man sows, that he will also reap.

GALATIANS 6:7 (RSV)

Part Five

RIPPLES
of
FAITH

*No ray of sunlight is ever lost, but the green
which it wakes into existence needs time to sprout,
and it is not always granted to the sower to live to see the harvest.
All work that is worth anything is done in faith.*
ALBERT SCHWEITZER

Not Too Broken to Be Fixed

Victor Fried

My family believed if something went wrong, it was always someone else's fault. I readily picked up this attitude and ran with it. Actually, when you think about it, it's not a bad plan. I was not responsible for any of my failures; they were always someone else's fault. I could feel anger toward the "responsible parties" rather than feeling inadequate myself.

At some point I asked myself, "Why are so many people out to get me?" The only logical answer was that even God hated me. So I returned the favor and hated God right back.

My belief that God hated me grew as the years passed, and I perceived each setback as further evidence that my belief was correct. I had heard it said that God works through people; seeing the number of people I thought were out to get me, I guessed it was true!

Having learned as a child to "solve" my problems by fighting, it's not surprising that as an adult I gradually fell deeper and deeper into a violent lifestyle. Yet strangely, I always hated myself for hurting people, especially if I hurt someone I cared about. As a result I gradually learned to stay away from anyone I cared about, and I became a loner. I knew that all I could do with any consistency was hurt people, so I tried to keep it to hurting only strangers.

Eventually I did discover something else I was good at: building custom furniture. But my inner rage continued to grow and so did the incidences of people apparently going out of their way to cause me grief. One weekend day while driving down a street in Kansas City, I noticed a man carrying an antique Queen Anne chair to a Dumpster in an apartment complex. I could see that the chair had a broken rung, a problem I could easily fix. That chair was worth money to me—something I desperately needed. So I quickly turned into the complex and stopped my car beside the Dumpster. As the man approached, I asked, "If you're going to throw that away, may I have it?"

"No." And he smashed it over the side of the Dumpster. I watched in disbelief as the old wood shattered on impact. Too stunned even to reply, I drove off.

What a complete and total lowlife, I thought to myself. *He didn't want it, but he would rather destroy it than give it to someone who could fix it and use it.* Once again, I had more evidence that God, using people, was out to get me.

Finally, when I was forty, I felt I had suffered all I could bear. I was tired—tired of failing, tired of fighting against the world, tired of living. Although I still had a strong fear of death, that fear was overpowered by a worse fear of life. I drove my car down along the Missouri River just outside Kansas City, parked, and walked downstream.

I was serious—deadly serious. I found a place where I could easily climb down to the water's edge and stood for a moment looking at the ice chunks floating past, taking one last look around before letting myself fall into the river. My life was nearly over, and all I felt was a sense of relief.

Then suddenly, unbidden, the memory of that man with the chair at the Dumpster came to my mind. I was looking at the rushing river that was about to relieve me of the burden of life, yet what I saw was that chair smashing into a thousand splintered pieces. Then a voice came from inside me or from right beside me—I cannot say which:

"If you're going to throw that away, may I have it?"

I knew that it was the voice of God. In a millisecond my mind flooded with images of the man I had been all my life, the people I had hurt, the destruction that lay behind me. Yet at that moment I knew beyond all doubt that God loved me—in spite of what I had done, because of who God is—and that his love was unconditional.

I fell to my knees and cried tears of shame, pain, and joy. At that moment I knew that I wanted to give my life to God. At the time I had no idea how I would do it, but I knew that if God could fix me and use me, I would not be like the man with the chair at the Dumpster.

On that cold wintry day on the bank of the Missouri River, circumstances caused me to become willing. In fact, as it turned out, all I had to do to give my life to God was to become willing: willing to listen, willing to do whatever God put in front of me, willing to trust that God would not give me a task beyond my abilities, willing to accept that God is more concerned about my welfare than I am, willing to recognize that everything I'd thought I knew could be wrong, willing to see the truth—even when the truth hurt—and willing to let go of my hate so my hands would be free to grasp love.

And when I fall short on all other counts, I remember that there is nothing that can keep the love of God from any person.

Storms make trees take deeper root.
CLAUDE MCDONALD

Rachel's Story

James Robison

It began in April 1999 as I sat in my home weeping over the senseless killings at Columbine High School in Littleton, Colorado. That tragedy was one of the darkest days in American history. Twelve students and a teacher lost their lives. As I watched the television coverage of the funeral of Rachel Scott, the first student shot, little did I realize how her life would touch my wife, Betty, and me—and hundreds of others.

Rachel was a dedicated follower of Christ, proclaiming her faith even in her last moments. Her pastor, Bruce Porter, confirms that there is firm testimony that Rachel was taunted for several minutes by her killers after she was wounded. In the end she proclaimed her love for Jesus moments before the fatal shot was fired.

Rachel often wrote in her diary about her relationship with the Lord. One year to the day before she died, she wrote these words: "I lost all my friends at school. Now that I've begun to walk my talk, they make fun of me…but it's all worth it to me. I am not going to justify my faith to them and I'm not going to hide the light that God has put into me. If I have to sacrifice everything, I will."

In the sorrowful days following the massacre at Columbine High, I called a pastor I knew and asked if some of us from my ministry could come to his church to help. We felt led by God to help minister to the families and others in the community affected by the shootings, just as we have done in response to tragedies in our own state.

There were several wonderful testimonies of faith from people whose lives were impacted by the Columbine massacre, and later we shared their stories on our television program, *Life Today.* It was during the taping of one of the programs that we first met Beth Nimmo and her husband, Larry—Rachel's mother and stepfather. They spoke lovingly of a daughter who sought to let her light shine for the Lord and of her promising future. As they shared about Rachel and her faith, they mentioned her desire to one day be a missionary to Africa. In fact, she had made plans to go to Africa as a short-term missionary the next summer. Learning of Rachel's interest in Africa, I asked Beth and Larry if they wanted to go with my wife and me on our next mission trip to Africa. They accepted in her memory; Rachel's dream to go to Africa was to be fulfilled by her mother and stepfather.

Our organization sponsors what we call a Mission Feeding, a life-saving outreach that gives people food and responsibility. This was a particularly challenging time for the Mission Feeding program. We had been caring for eighty-five thousand children and their families, and on this trip we learned that at least fifty new feeding centers in remote areas desperately needed food. Later a worker told me he had never seen such desperate hunger.

We visited a cemetery in Angola, near Benguela. Just a year earlier when we visited this area, we had rejoiced when we saw very few fresh graves. But this time the story was much different. We stood with Rachel's parents in the burial ground and were horrified to see hundreds of new graves. We learned that refugees were being driven from the interior of the country toward the coastline and that literally thousands were dying along the way. In that cemetery alone, 650 children had been buried just since April. As tears streamed down Beth's cheeks, she reminded us that Rachel had died in April, and she knelt among the graves of small children from six months to two years old. She saw little makeshift wooden crosses with the names of the children, their birth dates, and the date of their death scribbled on them. Most likely they perished from starvation or disease resulting from malnutrition.

Beth Nimmo stood on African soil and wept, knowing that her daughter was gone but God was fulfilling her dream. I will never forget that day and those circumstances. Through her tears she told us, "We want to do something to honor Rachel, and so we present this check to you to help stop what is going on here." What an incredible moment it was! Right there among the graves of children on dusty African soil, I knew that truly Rachel Scott did not die in vain.

Rachel never went to Africa, and yet the faith of a young high-school girl has touched her school, her community, her nation, and now touches the world.

What is lovely never dies, but passes into other loveliness.

THOMAS BAILEY ALDRICH

The Fall
of Humpty Dumpty

Wayne Holmes

> *Humpty Dumpty sat on a wall,*
> *Humpty Dumpty had a great fall.*
> *All the king's horses and all the king's men*
> *Couldn't put Humpty together again.*

During a stint as a children's pastor, I often spoke to children about spiritual concerns. One of my favorite object lessons entailed a bit of juggling. Now, I *can* juggle three items—but not without a few mishaps. For this particular object lesson, my obvious amateur status kept the interest level high and made the whole presentation more memorable, as I was to discover.

I had been asked to speak at back-to-back chapel services in a local Christian elementary school. Equipped with my juggling paraphernalia, my confidence was high. After all, I had presented this sermon to other audiences and, I thought, perfected it.

I began the routine by juggling scarves. Scarves, being soft and pliable, are easy to handle. They tend to float in the air, which allows the juggler a better chance to recover after a mistake, and even when the juggler grips them tightly, they tend to return to their original shape.

I told the children that scarves remind me of the type of person I want to be—easy to work with, more forgiving, able to rebound from the pressures of life.

After juggling the scarves for a few seconds, I put them aside and brought out a can of tennis balls, explaining that rubber balls are also an example of the type of person I want to be. They bounce back when dropped and will not cause injury if handled improperly.

I used the next item I juggled to illustrate the type of person I do *not* want to emulate. Billiard balls are hard and dense. If handled carelessly, they can hurt. They do not bounce back from mistakes as readily as tennis balls, and they are unforgiving objects that must be handled with caution.

The final trick in my repertoire was to juggle raw eggs, demonstrating another type of person I do not want to emulate. Eggs are hard on the outside but a gooey mess on the inside. One must be extremely careful when handling them, for they break easily. And once they've been mishandled, there's no chance of recovery. One mistake and the yolk is on you.

As I prepared to juggle the eggs, I stopped.

"Maybe I should put something on the floor, just in case I accidentally drop an egg," I announced, building my audience's anticipation as I fetched a plastic garbage can liner to cover the area beneath my feet and prepared to try again.

"Okay, here goes." But I paused again.

"Wait a minute. This is my favorite suit. I don't want anything to ruin it. Maybe I should put something over my pants."

I fetched a second garbage bag, stepped inside, pulled it over my trousers, and tucked the top inside my belt. My audience watched closely.

"Okay," I said. "Here goes."

Heads strained to see as the eggs began to fly. Now you must understand that as part of my lesson I always allow one to drop. This is what the kids want to see! Besides, it makes the lesson more memorable and quiets any scoffers who suspect the eggs are hard-boiled.

On this particular occasion, however, I did not have to feign incompetence. I allowed one of the eggs to get away from me—so much so that it missed the plastic liner and landed on the carpet. The kids loved it, of course, but the teachers didn't seem to see much humor in it, and I was embarrassed. I babbled a string of apologies and pleaded for help in cleaning the carpet before it was permanently stained. In fact, I felt so bad, I chose to do a completely different chapel lesson for the next group of kids. I felt like I had really blown it, like I was a failure.

But guess what? One student wrote, "Your chapel service yesterday was spectacular." Another said, "I'm going to ask you to come again, 'cause it was the most fun I ever had since 4th grade. I'm in 6th grade." Others even learned a thing or two. One student wrote, "I learned something about forgiveness," and another said, "I learned not to juggle eggs!"

None of the children in chapel that day will remember the eggs that didn't break. But they will remember the broken egg for a long time.

Think about it: That egghead Humpty Dumpty's only claim to fame was his unfortunate accident. One wonders why he was on the wall in the first place; he must have known he was courting disaster! Yet, defying common sense, Humpty teetered on the edge until there was no turning back. In an instant he crossed the line of security, plummeted to the earth, and came to an early demise. Why? Why did he push himself beyond the safety of the wall? Why did he risk life and limb (or in this case, white and yolk)? Why didn't he avoid the risk and opt instead for a long, healthy, secure life? Yet had he done so, he would have died in obscurity.

Of what value is an unbroken egg? An unborn chick cannot live indefinitely inside an egg. You and I can't eat an egg until it's removed from the shell. The fact is, an egg that is never broken is an egg that is wasted.

Likewise, a life that does not know a measure of brokenness is a life that may never reach its full potential. A life that has experienced its share of brokenness, on the other hand, is in a position to make an impact on the world.

The value of a life, in fact, is measured not only by its wholeness, but by the extent of its usefulness in its brokenness. This is not an easy concept to accept. We like our heroes and heroines to be knights in shining armor and princesses who wear glass slippers. But armor tends to get beaten and rusty, and glass slippers break under real pressure.

Understandably, we try to avoid the things that accompany brokenness—pain, suffering, and sorrow. However, when these things are unavoidable, we can choose how we will respond to them: We can try to put the pieces back together, pretend nothing happened, and go on with our life in a business-as-usual manner; or we can embrace our brokenness.

Denying our brokenness circumvents growth, learning, and the healing of the inner person. Instead of denying or ignoring pain, we must embrace it. Instead of running from brokenness, we must determine to learn from it. Pain has the potential to help us more than we ever dreamed possible.

So find the beauty in your brokenness. Learn to profit from your pain. And seek to share what you have learned with your fellow "eggheads."

God will not look you over for medals, degrees, or diplomas, but for scars.

PAUL E. HOLDCRAFT

Now This Is Music!

Renee Bondi as told to Colleen Edwards

I had such wonderful plans laid out for my life, and I seemed to be right on track with them. In fact, on that day in May 1988, it seemed nothing could possibly go wrong. I never suspected that within a month that day would seem like a different life, one lived by someone else altogether.

Vocal music had long been my life, but for years I'd felt called to be a teacher as well. When I was hired as the choral music teacher at San Clemente High School, the job looked like it would be a challenge, to say the least: There were only 18 students enrolled in the choir program. Through dedication and persistence, our ranks swelled to 150 in just two years. Lots of "cool kids" joined, and singing was suddenly an "in" thing to do. The music room became a place kids wanted to be, a place they belonged.

As much as I loved my kids, 1988 was to be my last year at San Clemente. I was engaged to be married in the summer and after the wedding would join my new husband in Denver. I'd made plans to pursue a master's degree in vocal performance at the University of Colorado in Boulder. But first I needed to accomplish one more thing with my choir: to see them stretch musically as far as they could.

As a final tribute to my students I entered our choir in an upcoming competition. This was no ordinary music festival. It was to be held in a huge performing arts center, with most of the top choirs of southern California competing. Dr. Howard Swan, known as the grandfather of choral music and considered the ultimate judge for choral competition, would be rating the participants.

My students gasped when I first told them of my musical selection for the competition. "Brahms?! But it's so *heavy.*" "And it's in *German!*" "Do you really think we can pull this off?!" I had selected a piece by Brahms because the music was passionate, complex, and would push our choir to its limits and test our musicianship.

"Gang, I know we can do this," I replied firmly. "You may not always get to choose the songs. But if you'll trust me, I know we are on the road to making some beautiful music."

The day of the competition arrived. We had worked long, hard, disciplined hours and had fun. Our relationships with each other had grown stronger. We knew that our goal of earning a good mark from Dr. Swan couldn't be reached without everyone working together. And now it was time to show our stuff.

Hundreds of guests filled the rows of seats beyond the blinding lights. Dressed in tuxedos and formal dresses, we walked onstage. The choir watched me expectantly, and I could tell they were nervous. Standing in front of them, I gave them the "thumbs up" and mouthed to them, "We can do this!"

Their harmonies were perfectly balanced. Their German was rich and authentic. The sopranos floated over the high notes, the boys' voices were full and robust. By the end we were in a trance. We had forgotten about the audience and the judge and were caught up in the making of great music. I brought the piece to a close with one small hand motion. The audience was silent for a full five seconds, then broke into thunderous applause.

We had nailed it! It was our best performance ever, and I could see on their proud faces that the kids knew it. But would the judge agree? The students headed toward the bus in a frenzy of excitement while I awaited the results. When I finally boarded the bus, the kids were overcome with anticipation. My stomach fluttered as I opened the rating sheet.

It read, "Now THIS is Brahms!" The rating next to the comment was SUPERIOR—the highest ranking possible. The students roared in celebration. I'd taken a risk that had paid off! I felt deep confidence and contentment.

One month later, on a Sunday evening, I got up from my kitchen table after preparing lessons for the upcoming week. I felt happy but drained. I was thinking about wedding details that needed attention, the impending move, and my many farewells. It was going to be an emotional time for me and for many of my students as well. I crawled into bed, exhausted.

Around 2:00 A.M., I suddenly woke up in midair, falling off the foot of my bed onto my head. As I hit the floor, I heard my neck crack. I found myself flat on my back with my feet in the closet and my head up against the dust ruffle. *What happened? How did I get here?* I thought sleepily as I tried to roll over and sit up.

It didn't work. Instead, I heard another *craaaaack* and felt a burst of pain. Resolutely, I tried to roll over to my other side. *Crrraaccck.* That shot of electrifying pain took my breath away. As I gasped for air, I knew that I couldn't get up. I needed help, but my roommate, Dorothy, was sound asleep upstairs. I tried to yell out, but the shout came out as a breathy whisper. I couldn't even talk!

She'll never find me! I'll lie here until morning! I tried not to panic.

Amazingly, within minutes the door opened. Dorothy had awakened from a deep sleep and felt compelled to come to my room. "Renee?" she asked, turning on the light. "Are you all right?"

"My neck is killing me," I whispered. "It's serious. Call the paramedics."

Seeing the distress in my eyes, she ran for help.

When I awoke in the hospital's intensive care unit, I was groggy and in tremendous pain. The doctor's deep, dark eyes were serious. He wasted no time mincing words.

"Renee," he said, "your neck is broken. Your fall has left you a quadriplegic."

"What exactly does that mean?" I asked.

"This means that you are paralyzed from the neck down. You'll never be able to walk, sit up, or move your arms or legs," he explained. "I also understand you are quite the singer. Your diaphragm has been severely compromised. You won't have the breath support to sing as you have in the past." He added gently, "I am very sorry."

I was crushed. All I had done was go to bed! How could I be paralyzed? Was I dreaming?

It's hard to stay in denial when faced by such overwhelming physical evidence. Next I tried to grasp the impact of the injury on my life—or what used to be my life. It was clear all my plans were as shattered as my vertebrae: I couldn't teach, I couldn't sing, and I certainly couldn't expect Mike to marry a quadriplegic when he'd proposed to a healthy woman.

My life was over. "God," I anguished, "this is not what I had in mind for my life! I can't do it! Why? Why couldn't you have given me an easier path?"

Although everyone around me had been lifting me up in prayer, it was hard for me to stay focused on anything, let alone a conversation with God. Every time I tried to pray, I would get distracted by my racing thoughts. But one night, in the early morning, I tried again. An old song came into my head: *Be not afraid, I go before you always.* And then I felt the Spirit say: *You may not always get to choose the songs, but if you put your trust in me, you'll surely make beautiful music.*

Did I have the same faith I required of my students?

My answer was hard-wrung. "Yes, Lord, I'll trust you, I'll trust you."

The first "song" he gave me was incredibly precious. Mike insisted on becoming my husband. He strengthened the resolve I had to teach again. The fight I might not have been able to make for myself became easier when I thought of God, Mike, and my future students. I even vowed to sing again.

Twelve years have passed, and God has been faithful. I gave birth to a beautiful baby boy. I've taught music at church, where I've been able to form three youth choirs. I've made three recordings of music for people who need courage, strength, and hope, like I did. I now travel nationally as a speaker and vocalist sharing God's faithfulness, even in times of great adversity.

No, my life is not at all what I'd planned. But every now and then I see the sweet harmonies and sweeping cascades of God's arpeggios all around me, and I think, *Now this is music!*

> *The LORD is my strength and my shield;*
> *my heart trusts in him, and I am helped.*
> *My heart leaps for joy*
> *And I will give thanks to him in song.*
> PSALM 28:7

Holy Ground

Fred M. Rogers

Fred Rogers, creator and host of the television program *Mr. Rogers' Neighborhood,* is also an ordained Presbyterian minister. While still a student at Pittsburgh Theological Seminary, he attended a different church each Sunday during the summer so that he could hear a variety of preachers.

One Sunday he heard what he felt was "the most poorly crafted sermon ever given." But when he turned to one of his friends who had attended the service with him, he found her in tears.

"He said exactly what I needed to hear," she told Rogers.

"That's when I realized that the space between someone doing his best and someone in need is holy ground. The Holy Spirit transformed that feeble sermon for her, and as it turned out, for me, too."

For we are God's fellow workers;
you are God's field, God's building.

1 CORINTHIANS 3:9

Pass It On

Kurt Kaiser

It only takes a spark to get a fire going,
And soon all those around can warm up in its glowing.
That's how it is with God's love, once you've experienced it:
You spread his love to everyone,
You want to pass it on.

What a wondrous time is spring— when all the trees are budding,
The birds begin to sing, the flowers start their blooming.
That's how it is with God's love, once you've experienced it:
You want to sing, it's fresh like spring,
You want to pass it on.

I wish for you, my friend, this happiness that I've found—
You can depend on him, it matters not where you're bound.
I'll shout it from the mountaintop, I want my world to know:
The Lord of love has come to me,
I want to pass it on.

It Only Takes a Spark

Cheryl Kirking

When I was fifteen, some friends invited me to attend a winter youth retreat at a nearby camp. I was eager to go along and participate in some teenage fun.

As soon as we arrived at the camp, we dumped our luggage off at our cabin and made our way to the main lodge, where a couple hundred youth had already gathered to hear the evening's speaker. My friends and I squeezed into a spare patch of floor near the back of the huge lodge. The crowd was already singing a rousing rendition of "Do Lord," led by a young man with a guitar.

Then something happened that changed my life. The songleader strummed the opening chords to the song "Pass It On" and invited us to join in. I had never heard the song before, but apparently almost everyone there had. It was beautiful! I was in awe of the powerful spirit of love that wrapped around us like a blanket as hundreds of voices sang together:

> *It only takes a spark to get a fire gong,*
> *And soon all those around can warm up in its glowing*
> *That's how it is with God's love, once you've experienced it:*
> *You spread his love to everyone,*
> *You want to pass it on.*

I felt the Spirit tugging at my heart, that still, small voice urging, *I want you to know my love so deeply that you can't help but want to pass it on to others. And to do that, you need to trust me. Let my will be yours.*

The song touched a place in my soul that had never been reached before.

Now I understood why my parents made us go to church. All the years of Sunday-school training, preparing for this moment, finally kicked in. The baby in the lowly manger; the Teacher who shared God's love yet suffered man's cruelty; the forgiving Savior who died for my transgressions; the God who gives life, forgiveness, hope, love. I wanted to shout, "I get it!" I had been trying to make myself "good enough" for God to accept; now I understood that God loves me as I am, flaws and all! I can never be "good" on my own. I need God, the source of all goodness, to do the changing in me. The words to the Lord's Prayer echoed in my mind: "Thy will be done." *Yeah, I get it, God! Thy will!*

When I returned home from that transforming weekend, I pulled out my guitar, which I hadn't played for months. I wrote my first song and haven't stopped writing since. It took another fourteen years for me to have the courage to actually sing my songs for others. I now see there was a reason for that—I needed time to grow. At the urging of my husband and my church, I began a full-time music ministry in 1989. That year I had the wonderful opportunity to hear Kurt Kaiser, the composer of "Pass It On," perform the song at a musician's conference.

I am constantly amazed that God has given me the privilege of singing my songs for others. I don't have an impressive voice, and my songs are simple. But I have learned that simple gifts are of no less value than seemingly impressive ones. God will use whatever gifts he has given you to, as the lyrics say, "spread his love to everyone." Maybe your gift is the ability to really listen to someone who needs to be heard. Or help someone with their taxes. Or mow a lawn, smile at the grocery clerk, tie a shoe. All it takes is a willing heart.

When I decided to compile this book, I contacted Kurt Kaiser. I wanted to thank him for the ripple effect his song has had on my life.

As the lyrics say, "It only takes a spark to get a fire going." But a spark needs something to ignite, something to fuel the fire. The years of church attendance that my parents insisted upon, the loving example I had witnessed in my family and my church family—these were the kindling that had been laid, waiting for the spark that would ignite my personal faith. The Spirit used music to reach my soul. For others he may use a glorious sunset, a mountaintop view, a baby's smile, a quiet touch from a friend.

He may use you. Are you available? It only takes a spark.

*Do not be afraid to use what talents you possess,
for how silent the woods would be if no birds
sang except those which sang best.*

HENRY VAN DYKE

A Song in My Heart

Roy Wayne Howard
as told to Jeannie S. Williams

Several years ago our gospel singing group, Freedom Ridge, gave a concert for a small church in a little Illinois town. We played and sang for about thirty minutes, and then I asked the pastor to come forward and lead the congregation in prayer. Just as the pastor started forward, an old man got up from the pew where he was sitting and approached the platform.

"I'd like to sing before the preacher comes," the old gentleman said. His voice was almost a whisper, and I had to lean forward to hear what he was saying. The pastor sat back down as I explained the request, and my band members picked up their instruments again.

"I'm ninety-seven years old and probably won't be on this earth many more years," the old man began to speak. His voice trembled, and I could see his hands were shaking. "I am about to do something I been wantin' to do for a long time. This young man here doesn't have any idea what this means to me...You see, I've never sang in front of a group of people before. Nope, never have...But tonight I have a song in my heart. My Lord put it there...and I'd like to sing it for you. That is, if I can get this here young man to help me out." He looked over at me and smiled. I stepped forward and asked him what song we were going to play. "Can you help me out with 'I'll Fly Away?'" he asked.

I was relieved because it was an old gospel favorite. I kicked off with the lead in a fast tempo and Jim, our bass player, followed with good loud rhythm. But I knew immediately something was not right. I realized the old man wasn't even listening to the band; he was several

97

beats behind. He was singing the song very slowly, softly. I had never heard "I'll Fly Away" sung that slow in my entire life!

I waved my arms at the band and they began to slow down too. We sang and played slower and slower until we finally matched our music with his rhythm. The band members finally quit trying to sing with the old man but continued to play very softly. When the music finally rested on the same beat as his voice we were in unison, and the song coming from the old man was the most beautiful sound I had ever heard.

Tears began to stream down his face as he sang the song God had put in his heart. My own eyes filled with tears as I listened to the old familiar words. I didn't want the song to end, but when the music stopped, the awesome power of the Holy Spirit filled the room. The entire congregation sat in awe. Many were wiping their eyes, while others lifted their hands to heaven in praise.

"I don't know anything about music," the old gentleman said quietly as he handed the microphone back to me, "but I sure do love that old song."

Many years have passed since that night, but I've never forgotten that old man and how sweetly he sang that song. He probably didn't know anything about music—but I can assure you that old man knows the Master who put the song in his heart.

A few can touch the magic string,
And noisy fame is sure to win them;
But alas for those who never sing,
But die with all their music in them.

OLIVER WENDELL HOLMES

Part Six

RIPPLES
of
COMFORT

*Sometimes our light goes out but is blown
into flame by another human being.*
ALBERT SCHWEITZER

A Special Birthday Party

Rochelle M. Pennington

Gramps was a talker from the day he was born, and by the time he was in his eighties, practice had certainly made perfect. Easy-flowing conversations always kept him in the thick of things, exactly where he liked to be.

His daily rounds led him through town in a predictable manner: post office, café, hardware store, grocery—pretty much in that order. He preferred getting his news from people rather than from the papers, something that could be accomplished easily enough while he was "out and about" among the locals. He would return home midafternoon, quite satisfied that he had a handle on the world: what was new, what was old, and what was in between.

This particular day was not unlike any other day. Gramps made his final stop at the grocery store to pick up a loaf of bread before heading home. That's where he spotted them—the nonlocals. A mother with two small children had just rounded the corner of the bread aisle.

There wasn't anything Gramps enjoyed quite so much as striking up small talk with someone he had never met before. Forgetting that he had been reaching for a loaf of bread, Gramps shifted gears from grocery shopper to public relations specialist. The process of de-strangerization took less than eight minutes, after which Gramps knew that the family had just moved to town, were living on Elm Street in the blue Cape Cod on the corner, were celebrating the father's birthday this afternoon, and had come to purchase a bouquet of balloons for the party.

"A birthday party, you say!" Gramps cheerfully exclaimed as he quickly joined their circle of anticipatory excitement. It was a nice place to be.

Always helpful, Gramps walked along with them to the back corner of the store, where the helium tank and balloon display were located. Soon a rainbow of colored balloons, inflated and tied together with curled ribbons, floated overhead. "Wait 'til Daddy sees this!" the children chirped in their sweet soprano voices.

Both Gramps and the little family were soon ready to check out. Since Mabel's register was open, they all filed into line: skipping girls in pink dresses first, mother with her white purse next, Gramps and his bread last of all.

Being a mother of seven and having purchased many dozens of balloon bouquets over the years herself, Mabel felt it her maternal duty to gently share some reminders.

"Such wonderful balloons you have!" she said to the girls. "Why, there's so many of them I should think they'd lift the both of you up together, just like Mary Poppins!" They giggled.

"Make sure you hang on tight," Mabel went on. "*Real* tight. Gramps told me you're on your way to a birthday party. We want those balloons to get there, right?" In response, four chubby little hands clenched the strings even more tightly.

Gramps and Mabel shouted departing greetings to the family as they left. "Have fun! Remember to hang on tight! We'll be seeing you soon!"

Placing his bread on the conveyor belt, Gramps continued to watch them through the large wall of windows as they walked outside. And no sooner had they gotten beyond the expansive overhang of the building than the little girls opened their clenched hands and the balloons flew away.

Gramps wailed, "Oh no!" as he went darting out the door. Upon reaching the family, he continued to lament. But no one seemed to hear him. His words were drowned out by the usual reaction of children in the presence of helium balloons set free: Little voices squealing, little hearts laughing, little hands clapping, and little feet jumping for joy as they watched the bouquet dance across the endless sky in freedom. And these little ones seemed extra exuberant.

Ah, youth, thought Gramps.

Touching their mother's shoulder gently, Gramps was going to offer to spring for the next bouquet. "Too bad about the balloons. They're supposed to be for their father."

Touching Gramps's shoulder gently in return, the young woman responded, "And he'll be receiving them anytime soon now…in heaven."

Never before—or since—had Gramps attended a birthday party quite so splendid.

> *Life is a voyage that's homeward bound.*
> HERMAN MELVILLE

Luke's Truck

Roberta L. Messner, Ph.D.

Eyes wide with terror peered at me from the hospital bed. "You must be Luke Hatten," I said as I scanned the name on his identification bracelet.

Late afternoon shadows flickered on the window like an anxious caller as the man's work-roughened hands nervously fingered a pamphlet lying on the overbed table. Its bold, red letters shrieked, "When You Have Cancer."

I cleared my throat uneasily. "I'm Roberta Messner, a registered nurse. Your doctor and wife thought it might be helpful if I visit you after you're discharged. It's all part of a special school project. If it's okay, I'll stop by Saturday."

Mr. Hatten stared blankly out the window at the winter sticks and stubble of the hospital grounds. In a couple of months, the now-barren grounds would be awash with the newness of spring—brave crocuses, vibrant azaleas, hyacinths in Easter-egg hues.

But this was the cancer ward, where time is measured in moments, not months.

Mr. Hatten's roommate caught up with me by the elevator. "You've got your work cut out for you, Nurse," he stated flatly. "They say it's terminal. Ever since Luke got his sentence, he walks the floor all night. Told me, 'I can't sit for long. When I sit, I think.' The tension is so thick you could cut it with a chain saw."

I felt defeated from the start. *Why didn't I sign up for the prenatal clinic project?* I mumbled to myself. Here it was the eve of spring, with the promise of new life, and my patient was dying. How would I ever know how to help him?

On Saturday morning, a short, stout woman met me at the door of the Hatten's tidy rural cottage. "I'm Ida. Do come in," she said as she tugged at the hem of her cotton apron.

Luke sat in a frayed wing chair in a corner of the living room. He forced a smile. I fumbled with the buttons on my lab coat, then knelt beside him, leaning forward to admire the tabletop display of photos. "Been married forty-two years," he muttered. "Never had any young 'uns."

Just two weeks before, Luke had undergone surgery for cancer of his colon. But the tumor hadn't been discovered soon enough. Now the relentless disease had spread throughout his body. Once a hard-working, jack-of-all-trades handyman, a now-weary Luke clutched his abdomen in a spasm of pain. *Lord, help me know what to do,* I silently prayed.

"Luke just took a pain pill," Ida explained. "Why don't we have some coffee out in the kitchen while the medicine takes hold? I just took a cobbler out of the oven. Made with last summer's black-berries."

I followed Ida to the gingham-curtained kitchen window. A look of desperation stole across her deeply lined face. "This is all such a shock," she sobbed. "He worked so hard at any odd job he could find. Always tinkerin' on something. And just when he thought he was ready to retire, this happens."

Ida bit her lip as she twisted her worn wedding band around her finger, then pointed to the shining red truck in the driveway. "He wanted that truck so bad. Drove it straight from the showroom over to the clinic. His belly had been painin' him a little, but we never dreamed it was…cancer. Next day the Doc just cut him open and sewed him right back up. I'm trying to hold up for him, but I don't know how I'll ever make it. Luke did it all—I don't even have a driver's license."

I walked back into the living room. "That's quite a truck you have out there, Luke," I said.

"Never even got to show it to the crew down at the hardware store," came his faint words. "Doc says I can't drive. I'm on too many pills."

"Sometime when you feel up to some fresh air and exercise, I'd love to take a look at it. My husband has a truck too, but it's an old clunker."

Luke's tired brown eyes lit up. "Had old junk heaps myself all of my life before. Always kept hopin' to get a new one. Then I did…just before this thing hit." He struggled out of the chair and pressed a kiss to Ida's plump cheek. "Gimme my coat, hon."

With marrow-deep determination, Luke led me past the white picket fence and out to the driveway. He pointed to a row of brittle, lifeless bushes. "There'll be yellow blossoms like you never did see on them come spring. Sure would like to see spring come one more time." Luke dusted the glistening truck with the sleeve of his plaid flannel jacket, then cautiously peeped in the windows as if it belonged to someone else.

"Would my husband ever love this beauty!" I exclaimed. "Just look at those chrome bumpers and those black leather seats."

"Well, climb up in 'er and have a seat," Luke urged. He positioned himself at the steering wheel and reached in his pocket for his keys. "Feels funny not havin' a floorboard full of old rags and oil cans," he chuckled.

"Better start it up to charge the battery," I suggested.

Luke turned the key in the ignition. "Gotta let it run a minute to lube the engine," he explained, honking the horn with the fervor of a three-year-old.

A neighbor pecked on the window. "Hey Luke, what's a pretty, young nurse doing in that there truck of yours?" he chided.

If my strait-laced professor could see me now, I thought wryly. Still, my stomach was one big knot. What do you say to someone who is dying? My education, I now recognized, had been long on generalities and short on specifics.

Luke toyed with the power seats, the electric mirrors, the quartz clock, the heater. My idle hands longed for a stethoscope. A thermometer. Anything to avoid the inevitable. But all of my gadgets were packed in my nurse's satchel in the Hatten's living room.

"How'd you ever decide on the color, Luke?" I asked, opting for small talk.

"Same color as the bike I got the Christmas I turned seven. Pa made me wait 'til after supper to ride it up the holler. Seemed like forever."

I soon discovered Luke was a different man in the driver's seat of his new truck. Strong. In control. In his own private world. And finally opening up to me.

"One day I was drivin' this truck off the car lot," he said softly, "and the next thing I knew they were sendin' a nurse to help me die." I nodded and reached for his hand. "Doc says I don't have long. I gotta put things in order, Nurse. I'm tellin' you this 'cause I don't wanna worry Ida."

I continued to visit Luke several times each week. I'd find him waiting in the driver's seat of the truck with a thermos of Ida's coffee and two mugs, anticipating our appointed visit. We talked freely of our shared faith, his fear of dying and leaving Ida alone, God's promise of eternal life. As Luke learned to face his pain—not run away from it—he grew more peaceful, even in the face of death. After our "truck talks," we'd head back to the kitchen where Ida waited. There we'd discuss the details of Luke's care and help Ida begin to plan for an uncertain future.

On Palm Sunday, I attended the morning worship service at church before checking on Luke. The pastor spoke about how Jesus became a man so that we could know God. He closed the sermon by recounting the story of Jesus facing death in the Garden of Gethsemane. Jesus had told his disciples, "My soul is exceeding sorrowful, even unto death: tarry ye here, and watch with me" (Matthew 26:38, KJV). Even Jesus had not wanted to face death alone.

That afternoon I found Luke leaning on Ida beside a budding

forsythia bush. His old black leather belt curled about him, gathering his trousers in loose folds, the unneeded length of perforated leather dangling at his side. He handed me some freshly cut branches, wrapped in wet paper towels and newspapers. "Put these in a jug of water when you go home and they'll take root. Someday you'll have a yard full of forsythias." I smiled, but deep down I doubted his wisdom. With what sorry little I knew about gardening, I was sure that a budding branch had a slim chance of ever taking root.

Over the next few days, Luke's condition rapidly worsened. At our last visit, he lay ashen and listless, his breathing rapid and labored. I leaned over to give him a hug. "I'm not afraid...anymore," he whispered. "Jesus is right here...reachin' his arms out to me. I'll live again...just like my Lord."

Luke died that evening, and I drove right over to be with Ida. "Oh, how I'll miss him," she wept. "But how could I want to drag my Luke back down to this old earth? He's livin' with Jesus. One day I'll see him again."

As I left the Hatten's home, I paused by Luke's truck and gazed into the window, studying the empty seats where the two of us had so often sat. The air was fragrant with the scent of spring flowers wafting in the gentle breeze. With the sleeve of my sweater, I buffed the red gem as Luke would have done, then lifted the windshield wipers to release a dusting of golden yellow forsythia blossoms. I pondered the lesson I'd learned—a lesson not taught in any classroom: If we are to really make a difference in the lives of others, we have to meet them where they are and feel their pain, just as Jesus did.

I might never have known the real Luke in his bewildering, antiseptic hospital room. In *my* secure environment. There in the rush of things, I might have been tempted to pat his hand, offer a trite reassurance, and go on about my duties.

But sipping coffee in that truck—Luke's Garden of Gethsemane—the barriers were broken, and two strangers experienced the promise of Easter.

The image has been etched in my memory for nearly a decade now. And lest I ever forget it, I'm reminded each spring by my yard full of Luke's forsythias.

> *Our Lord has written the promise of resurrection, not in books alone, but in every leaf of spring-time.*
>
> MARTIN LUTHER

Love, Leo

Doris Delventhal as told to B. J. Connor

It wasn't fair! At the age of fifty-nine, my devoted husband, Leo—seldom ever sick—was diagnosed with acute leukemia. Twenty-three days later, just before our thirty-fifth wedding anniversary, he died. We had counted on so many more years together; we didn't have enough warning!

The daughter of a pastor, I couldn't remember a time when I hadn't felt close to God—until then. I wanted to cling to God, but I was so bitter that he would allow somebody as strong as Leo to die and leave behind someone as emotionally fragile as I was. Well-meaning friends gave me a print of Jesus welcoming a man into heaven with open arms. Sometimes I put it out of sight and ranted at God, "You've had Leo long enough! I need him more than you do!"

Leo and I had truly been one, and I felt ripped apart when he was gone. Another widow told me it would be three years before I began to feel whole again. "Lord, will the pain always be this intense?" I anguished. "I need to feel your love! I need to feel Leo's!"

I lived on automatic pilot, going to my nursing job, coming home to my Leo-less house. Every problem seemed overwhelming. One morning I saw ants in the kitchen; Leo used to get rid of any ants. I grabbed a broom and jabbed at them futilely, growing angrier and angrier, screaming, "Leo, where are you? You belong here!"

I flung open the back door and wailed into my suburban back-yard. A neighbor rushed over. "Is anything wrong?"

"No…I just have to scream…" And I crumpled at the enormity of my loss.

Leo and I had grown to love each other deeply, but we weren't really in love on our wedding day in 1956; we hardly even knew each other. Poor, dear Leo. We married unaware that we were opposites. He was immaculate—almost perfect!—and assumed his nurse wife was also. But cobwebs didn't faze me. He loved classical music; I fell asleep at the first concert he took me to. He was a gourmet cook; I rotated ten recipes. He was reserved; I hugged spontaneously.

Our first years of marriage, Leo was not demonstrative. I desperately needed to hear him say "I love you," but he couldn't bring himself to say the words. Instead he'd say, "I like you—isn't that enough?"

After we'd been married about twenty years, we attended a marriage renewal retreat. The leaders encouraged us to write each other a love letter, mail the two letters in about a month, read them, and hide them to rediscover later. Leo wrote a beautiful letter full of words he found difficult to say aloud. From that time on, he had no trouble telling me he loved me.

But now he was gone.

I couldn't bear to part with Leo's belongings. Any scrap of paper with his handwriting on it—even doodling—was precious to me. A graphic-arts professor, he was a man of many other interests as well. I spotted on his desk the conductor's baton our three children and I had given him because he loved to conduct the invisible orchestras of his Bach and other tapes. I cried at that. I cried at every memento of his love for sailing and photography. A new wave of grief assaulted me with each reminder.

At one point I went to our room and splashed some of Leo's cologne on me so our bed would smell like him. I glanced down wistfully at our pillows. Leo and I used to clip out cartoons and leave them on each other's pillow. One of my last ones to him was a woman kneeling by a bed praying, "Dear God, make Mr. Perfect do just one thing wrong!"

We had lots to tease each other about. Because my purse had been stolen twice, I was obsessive about keeping it nearby. Leo and the kids said they were going to have "Where's my purse?" engraved on my tombstone.

Two years went by, and I screamed less and less. One day I opened a cookbook and found a valentine from Leo that I had used as a bookmark. Another day, while shopping, I saw a sailboat-shaped picture frame that reminded me of my beloved sailor and shutterbug. I bought the frame, put it on the TV and inserted one of Leo's spectacular sunsets. I gazed fondly, not weeping.

Another day I was going through the pockets of Leo's blazer, finally able to give it away, and found in the breast pocket a cartoon: archaeologists, unearthing a mummy with a purse, exclaimed, "It is! It is! It's the mummy's purse!" I laughed out loud, knowing Leo had intended to put this on my pillow.

A realization startled me: A reminder of Leo had brought not tears but laughter.

Shortly afterward I was cleaning out a cardboard-lined dresser drawer where I keep scarves. I glimpsed a long envelope under the cardboard and felt a surge of warmth at the familiar curve of Leo's handwriting. I shivered. It took my breath away. This was the letter Leo had written to me after the couples' retreat fourteen years before! I eagerly dug out the sheet of paper, my eyes devouring the words: *Dearest Doris...*

Leo quoted the poet Shelley, "One word is too often profaned/ For me to profane it," and then went on to say, *I truly do love you in all of the true meaning of the word—even if I am negligent or hesitant to say it. I love you. We are as one, and I must put forth the effort to make this a more complete oneness.... We were united in Christ's name and together we will grow in Christ's Love. Amen. Let it be so. With Everlasting Love—Leo (Just me).*

I was ecstatic! I needed this affirmation so badly that I clutched the letter to me and carried it from room to room, stopping every now and then to reread its words—words I don't think I could have handled right after Leo's death but ones that brought healing now. I folded the letter carefully and tucked it into my ever-present purse to open often. Just reading it makes me smile.

I still feel incomplete. But I also feel surrounded by God's and Leo's love. When something reminds me of Leo, there's a little less grief and a little more gratitude for what we had. My eyes get watery, but I can control it better now.

And sometimes I even laugh.

Over every mountain there is a path, although it may not be seen from the valley.

JAMES D. ROGERS

Loyalty

Dennis Myers

That Friday, January 19, 1962, was a cold, dreary winter day on the
Midwest farm. Homesteaded more than a hundred years earlier, the
farm was not much different than it had been for the past ten decades.

After morning chores, Papa sat down to write a letter to his
youngest child—a daughter, now living and working in the city. She
wasn't that far away—less than an hour's drive—but due to the se-
verity of the winter, it had been some time since she'd been home to
the farm. Papa wrote:

> Dear Daughter:
>
> You spoke about the weather; it is fine. The chiggers
> are not bothering me, the flies are not on the cattle. When
> I am sitting on the porch swing, I don't have to think
> about mowing the lawn or the weeds in the garden. We
> would like to see you but don't try to come home until
> the weather gets better. Wendell brought our groceries
> out yesterday. We've had our car out once since the middle
> of December. The cold has not bothered us as we have
> plenty of gas and wood for the cook stove. Don't know
> when you will get this as we don't get our mail regular.
> Mrs. Wetherell got stuck coming from work Tuesday
> evening and had to be pulled out. Hope you can read this,
> as my pen don't go where I want it to.
>
> With love, Papa

Mama slipped a companion letter in the same envelope, with additional comments about the snow and warnings to stay off the roads. After writing about not being out of the house or having visitors for several weeks, she ended,

> I want to see you so bad but don't take any risks for me. I think about your Aunt Nellie often, but I know she's better off where she is. I think of when we were little girls at home and playing house, but maybe it won't be too long for me to see her.
>
> My love to you, Mama

It was midmorning when Papa bundled up and took the letter to the street-side mailbox. Writing about the supply of wood for the cookstove made Papa think about the amount of firewood they had in the house. Too much would be an invitation for mice to take nest, but too little could mean a trip to the outbuilding in even worse winter weather. He headed for the stock of wood some two hundred yards behind the old farmhouse.

Papa cleaned several small logs, gathered the firewood in his arms and began the walk back to the house. At seventy-eight, he was not as limber as he'd been a few years ago. Walking down the lane from the outbuilding to the house, Papa's companion, a large, beautiful collie, pranced along by his side. They were inseparable. They worked together as a team on the farm, each with their own chores.

Suddenly Papa felt a pain like he had never known. Dropping the wood, he grabbed his chest. His knees buckled, and he slowly fell to the ground. Within seconds he was dead. Two hours later a neighbor passed by the house and saw something unusual near the sidewalk in front of the house. It was Papa. Lying on top of him, trying his best to keep his master warm, was his collie. His loyal friend!

Little did Papa realize that the letter he had penned to his daughter earlier in the day would be his last communication with her. She received the letter in the mail two days later. It brought tears to her eyes as she read it.

The daughter in this story is my mother. Today she has reached the same age her papa was then—and it still brings tears to her eyes as she opens the envelope to read his last letter just one more time. One more time, after hundreds of times. It also warms her heart to think of the collie comforting his master. Where else should a loyal friend be?

No one is useless in this world who lightens the burden of it for anyone else.

CHARLES DICKENS

The Flag

Teresa Griggs

It had been almost three years since my daughter Mallory's death. I missed her every day, but on holidays her absence was even more painful. Mallory had loved holidays, as most children do.

The Fourth of July was one of her very favorite times of the year. We live in a small town that still celebrates with a huge fireworks display, and each year our family and friends gather in a certain spot at the end of the day to enjoy the festivities. As the holiday approached that first year after Mallory's death, I felt it would be just too difficult for me to go to the fireworks show that evening. I could see in my mind Mallory's glowing face admiring the fireworks, the sparkle in her eyes from the flashes as each one went off; I could hear her squeals of delight. I did not want to ruin the fun for everyone else; maybe it would be best if I stayed home.

"Help me, Lord," I prayed on the morning of the Fourth. "Help me know the best thing to do in this situation." The study Bible I was currently using wasn't in its place; I must have carried it to another room or somehow misplaced it. On the bookshelf nearby was my old Bible. I picked it up and opened it, and a small sheet of paper fell at my feet.

It was a picture Mallory had drawn for me on the back of a church bulletin: the American flag. "To Mom," she had written across the page.

I hadn't used that Bible for a long time. Why on this day, the Fourth of July, did I decide to pick it up? Why did I not simply walk into the other room and find my other Bible? Was it a coincidence?

I don't think so. I think God was comforting me. Reminding me that Mallory is still a part of our family holidays—and still a part of our lives. Her memories are warm and wonderful. I don't have to run from them, and with God's help I can even embrace them. This Fourth of July and every one after, I will remember my daughter with love.

In the morning, O LORD, you hear my voice;
in the morning I lay my requests before you
and wait in expectation.

PSALM 5:3

A Little Reassurance

Wendy Dunham

It is 1:00 A.M. and my seven-year-old's voice breaks the night silence.

"Mom," she whispers forcefully from upstairs. Then, only a bit louder this time, "Mom?"

I slowly roll out of bed, knowing it's not an emergency—I would have heard "MOM!" for a real emergency. I stumble through the nighttime maze to reach the stairway. At the base of the stairs, I look up and see her silhouette: baby-doll jammies, shoulder-length braids.

"What's the matter, Erin?" I ask.

"I have to go to the bathroom, but there's a moth in there and he's scaring me."

"It's all right," I reassure her. "He won't bother you. He's sleeping."

Having no concept of the time gone by since her bedtime, Erin asked, "And what are you doin'?"

"I was sleeping too," I say.

"But did you already check on me?" One of my many nighttime duties. '

"No," I explain, "Daddy checked on you. I was very tired."

"Oh. He's home from his meeting already?"

"Yes, he's home, and he's sleeping too."

"Oh, okay. Mommy, I love you." She blows me a kiss, and the silhouette scampers away, braids bouncing.

I backtrack through the darkened maze and get back in bed. I can't sleep. Thinking about Erin, I'm struck with the correlation between my relationship to her and God's relationship to me. I imagine how I must appear to him sometimes.

"God?" I whisper. "Are you there?"

"Yes, I'm here," he answers. "I'm always here."

"What are you doing?"

"I'm watching over you. One of my many jobs."

"Oh," I say. "Thanks, God. It's nice to know that, because sometimes life can get a little scary down here. Good night, God. I love you."

"I love you too," he reassures me.

I smile and drift back to sleep.

Cast all your anxiety on him because he cares for you.

1 PETER 5:7

Part Seven

RIPPLES
of
COURAGE

People who pray for miracles usually don't get miracles...
But people who pray for courage,
for strength to bear the unbearable,
for the grace to remember what they have left
instead of what they have lost,
very often find their prayers answered.
Their prayers help them tap hidden reserves of faith and courage
that were not available to them before.
HAROLD S. KUSHNER

New World

Kathleen Ruckman

This is a true account of the journey taken by Kathleen's grandmother, who, with her eight children, traveled across the ocean from Czechoslovakia to Ellis Island, New York, in 1926. Kathleen remembers her grandmother telling this story many times on Sunday afternoons as Kathleen and her siblings and cousins gathered around the kitchen table at Grandma's house. The author's father is one of the triplets who made the journey. Kathleen tells the story through her grandmother's eyes.

"I've lost all track of time," Suzanna said in a tired voice as she leaned against the railing on the deck. "How many days have we been at sea?"

Ondrej, her oldest son, counted the pencil marks on a small wooden crate.

"Today is day twelve," he answered. "I've a mark for each sunset."

"Then we'll arrive tomorrow at Ellis Island," Suzanna said, her voice regaining strength. "The captain said thirteen days until February 22nd."

"That's if a storm doesn't take us off course," reminded thirteen-year-old Julka, Ondrej's twin sister. "There's something strange in the air."

Suzanna buttoned her black woolen coat closer to her chin. Her high-laced boots stopped just above her ankle. Thick, fuzzy gray socks peeked between the boots and her long black dress.

"We'll all be kings and queens in America!" said an old woman standing next to Suzanna. "The streets are lined with gold, you know," she clamored on.

"We'll know when we get there," Suzanna replied absently. She was scanning the crowd for her eight children. Hearing a whistling sound, she knew that Samuel, nearly four, was nearby. And if Samuel was there, so were his triplet brothers and the twin two-year-old boys. They usually stuck together. Hanka, the eldest of the eight, helped make sure of that.

Passengers bundled up in extra blankets rather than face their air-less steerage quarters below. Suzanna's milky skin took on a pink glow as she tightened her kerchief against the wind. Then she held on to the railing and looked out to sea. Tears filled her eyes.

"What's the matter, Mama?" Hanka asked, "Do you miss Czech-oslovakia so much?"

"I do miss the Tatras and the Danube," Suzanna answered, "but America will have new mountains and new rivers. It's my other three children…" she went on, wiping the tears from her eyes, remember-ing her three children who had died of diphtheria. "They were born there and died there." She sighed. "Part of me is still there."

"But Papa lived!" interrupted Hanka. "Papa got well!"

Suzanna lifted her chin as her spirits lifted too for a moment. She thought of her husband, Jano, waiting in America.

A needle-fine rain began to fall, blown sideways by the wind.

"I'm getting all wet!" squealed Palko, one of the triplets. His little brown dress flapped as the wind blew harder and the sky turned gray-green.

"All below deck!" a crewman shouted as weary passengers looked up to the sky and out at the sea. "The woman with all of the children first!"

"Come, children!" Suzanna said, quickly gathering her family to seek refuge in the steerage quarters below. But the deck was so crowded they could hardly walk.

Wind-chilled travelers packed together like sheep as they herded down the steps behind Suzanna. The wind and rain stung their faces, and frightened children cried as the boat rolled with the waves. Black clouds hovered low, and it looked as if nighttime was near. Yet it was only noon.

"I can't breathe down there!" whined Jano, a triplet, as Suzanna coaxed him down the last step.

The steerage quarters were stifling. Passengers huddled in corners or knelt on the floor as the sea rushed and whipped, attacking the ship. Trunks and crates fell from shelves, and frantic immigrants crawled to gather their treasures. And Samuel wasn't whistling.

"When will we get there? When? When?" cried Palko. Suzanna could only stroke his head.

The ship was like a cradle out of control. Babies cried as hammocks rocked wildly and tables collapsed. Suzanna and her children found a nook against the wall and clung to each other. Through the porthole they could see the crashing sea. Berti and Robert, the baby twins, hid their faces in Suzanna's coat while she prayed softly in Slovak. A Russian Jewish father pulled out a book of Psalms from a battered trunk and began to read, what little he could, out loud. Frightened immigrants embraced their loved ones as the unexpected storm continued. Surely it would be worth it all when they got to America.

Finally the storm died, and the ship settled into the sea to rest. No one said a word.

Although she had eight of her own to care for, Suzanna helped carry buckets of water to other passengers for drinking and washing. She kneeled down to help someone else's weary grandmother. That made Julka think of the words she often heard her mother say.

"Mamma says when you kneel down, and you're a servant, you're looking up—into the face of God," Julka said. "She says we ought to love one another," she told her twin.

The passengers climbed back up on deck to escape the muggy compartment. Faces lighted with anticipation once again as the sky cleared and the sun broke through. It was late afternoon. Another sunset.

Morning came. A sea gull followed the ship that day, and the journey was almost over.

"Help me get the sailor dresses out of the bedrolls," Suzanna told her daughters. Hanka and Julka unrolled the feather tick and pulled out five little dresses, appropriate attire for little boys in 1926 Czechoslovakia. They were blue with small black polka dots.

"Mama made these special for America!" Hanka told her little brothers, the triplets and the twins, as she straightened their collars and shined their shoes with the hem of her skirt.

For the first time in days, weary faces radiated hope. Even the crowded steerage compartment, once solemn, awakened with laughter. Amid the banging and gathering of crates and suitcases, a German father sang aloud in a deep baritone.

At last the ship passed through the narrows and entered the harbor, approaching Ellis Island. Passengers crowded the decks and cried as they saw the Statue of Liberty, and five little sailors clapped their hands!

The ship bumped and jarred the dock. The immigrants cheered and embraced each other. Crewmen appeared and began directing people and helping with belongings. Once again, Suzanna was led to the front of the line with her children. The triplets and twins followed her like little ducklings, and the three older children walked behind.

But before they got to the end of the gangplank, a tall man in a uniform shook his head with compassion and said, "Tomorrow."

Eventually the captain made an announcement to the confused passengers. "There's been a delay. We can't get off the ship. Today is George Washington's birthday. Ellis Island is closed until tomorrow."

"Who's George Washington?" Samuel asked, looking up at his mother. Surely this was a new land, a new heritage, a new name to learn.

Even such a disappointment couldn't crush the immigrants' spirits for long. They crowded the decks and looked out at their new land. Some laughed. Some cried. Some closed their eyes in silent prayer. Even the man who people said never smiled, whose face had been worn and wrinkled from years of farm work, looked at the coastline, wiping his tears. The immigrants stayed on the anchored ship one more day, the longest day of all!

"I'm going to get good work in America," a man told his family in Italian.

"You will have a good education in America," a grandmother reassured her grandchildren in Polish

"We'll soon see Father!" Suzanna said to her children. Then she told them in Slovak about the steel mill where Father worked and where they would live in Pennsylvania.

Very few slept that night, and the chattering went on for hours. Yet, amid the sounds of different lands, one word was the same on all tongues: "America!"

The things that the flag stands for were created by the experience of a great people. Everything that it stands for was written by their lives.
WOODROW WILSON

Angels Among Us

Cheryl Kirking

August 16, 1999, began as an ordinary day for Jill Cook, a sixty-seven-year-old crossing guard for the Polk County sheriff's office in Lakeland, Florida. But that changed in an instant.

While helping eight-year-old Tony Stringer and his sister Amber, ten, across the street, Jill was startled by the sound of screeching tires. She turned to see a pickup truck barely five feet away, heading straight for Tony. Without hesitation, Jill put herself between Tony and the speeding truck, knocking Tony out of the way. Taking the full impact, Jill was thrown up onto the roof, hitting the windshield before being tossed to the asphalt. She sustained numerous injuries, including five broken ribs, a broken leg, knee, pelvis, and hip. It is unlikely that slender young Tony would have survived the impact of the full-sized truck, which was estimated to be speeding at forty-six miles per hour.

"I was just doing my job," says Jill, "but the Lord was there." The children's mother, Christine Stringer, witnessed the entire incident from her backyard and says, "*Hero* is a big word, but not big enough for her. She was Tony's guardian angel that day."

> *Greater love has no one than this, that he lay
> down his life for his friends.*
>
> JOHN 15:13

Determined to Be Heard

Cheryl Kirking

Whoever says "Children should be seen and not heard" hasn't met Jennifer Danilee Turner.

One fall day while riding the bus to school, twelve-year-old Jennifer daydreamed as she looked out the window. As the bus crossed a bridge, she noticed a pickup truck down by the stream below. She could see only a small portion of the truck from her vantage point, as the bulk of it was under the bridge. Troubled, she told the bus driver to stop. The bus driver, of course, had a responsibility to his young passengers and couldn't stop on the busy highway.

Jennifer couldn't stop thinking about the truck, sensing that something wasn't right. It didn't belong there. When she got home, she asked her mother to go check on it, but her mother assured her it was probably nothing. Jennifer looked for the truck the next day as she rode the bus to school. It was still there. Still troubled, she told several adults about it. But no one seemed to share her concern.

Two days later, Jennifer and her grandfather, mother, and brother, Travis, were traveling home from Travis's football game. Although Jennifer couldn't see the truck, she insisted her grandfather stop to check on it. "I told her to forget about it," her grandfather, Massie Liggan, explains. "I said probably somebody had been down there fishing. Besides, it was soggy and muddy, as it had rained the past several days. And there was nowhere to stop close by on that busy road. We'd have to hike back a quarter mile after we parked just to take a look." But Jennifer was not going to be ignored again. "Something just pulled at my stomach that something wasn't right," she says.

"She threw a real fit," her grandfather recounts. "She said, 'Pa Pa, if you don't stop, I'm going to be mad at you the rest of my life!' Well, I finally said, 'All right, I'll stop, just to show you there's nobody down there.'"

He parked the car, and they began to hike back to the bridge. "Look, there *is* a truck!" Jennifer's mother exclaimed. As they trekked toward it, calling out to see if anyone was inside, they saw a hand wave weakly out of the passenger side window. When they reached the truck, they discovered a man, so weak and dehydrated from four days and three nights without food or water he could barely talk. An ambulance was called, and he was rushed to the hospital.

John Muller had been just a few hours from death. His potassium level, which affects the heartbeat, had become dangerously low from dehydration, and his heart would have failed had he not been found soon. In addition he had suffered a broken nose, two broken ribs, and a collapsed lung. After receiving medical attention, he had the strength to tell how he came to be stranded for three days in the truck by the stream.

John had been driving to his home in DeQueen, Arkansas, from the Little Rock airport when he felt a sudden cramp in his left leg, followed by massive spasms in his back. He had experienced back pain before, but this pain was so gripping that he passed out. His truck went out of control but miraculously avoided hitting the abutment of the bridge or any trees. It landed on the bank by the stream, just far enough under the bridge that it wasn't visible to passing cars.

When John regained consciousness, he tried to get out of the truck, but every time he moved, the pain would hit him with such intensity he would pass out again. Three days passed, and his wife, Paula, had no idea where her husband was. Because airline records confirmed he had, indeed, flown into Little Rock, it was assumed he was somewhere between Little Rock and his home in DeQueen. The sheriff's department printed fliers with John's photograph and began a full-scale search. The couple's sons and nephew had also come to join in the search, combing every strip of road between the airport and DeQueen. They had driven over the bridge at least twenty times, but because there were no marks on the guardrail and because the truck wasn't visible from the road, no one saw it.

No one, that is, except Jennifer, whose vantage point from the bus—higher than a car—allowed her to see a small portion of the wayward truck as she gazed, daydreaming, out the window at just the right moment.

Jennifer was awarded the Good Samaritan award by the De-Queen Sheriff's Department, and the story has been featured on national TV programs, including *Dateline*, *Oprah*, and *It's a Miracle*. But Jennifer discounts the courage she showed by refusing to back down when no one would listen to her. "I'm no hero," she insists. "God just used me to help find Mr. Muller. It was all part of God's plan."

But John Muller says, "She's my angel on earth."

An angel who was determined to be heard.

Perseverance is a great element of success. If you only knock long enough and loud enough at the gate, you are sure to wake up somebody.
HENRY WADSWORTH LONGFELLOW

Victory over the Pole

Nancy Zastrow

The thirty-foot pole stretched straight up like a telephone pole, tall and intimidating, and we were told to climb it.

Why would I climb a pole if I didn't have to? The truth was, I didn't want to. But this pole stood in my way—representing a barrier between God and me, between the world and me, perhaps between me and the rest of my life.

I had just completed a class that encouraged individuals to move from their comfort zone to their stretch zone. The lessons we had learned in the classroom were now going to be applied experientially. The idea was that taking part in such an exercise, called "Challenge by Choice," would create a model for life.

The thirty-foot pole occupied a notable spot on the challenge learning course. The facilitator explained that we were to climb the pole—outfitted all the way up with heavy metal staples to create a "ladder"—mount the disk that was attached at the top, turn around and face our group—and jump.

We would wear harnesses, and our suspension would be controlled by trained course technicians, who would manage the belay lines attached to the harness. Our fellow team members would operate the belay ropes that would lower us safely to the ground. And, our instructor reminded us, we could stop at any point; the purpose of the exercise was to challenge us to take just one step more than we normally felt comfortable taking.

For whatever reason, I was willing to give it a try.

For me, climbing the pole was the easy part; it took only seconds.

But as I approached the top, I saw that the disc mounted there was only the size of a pizza pan. Surely this was a mistake! My feet were bigger than that!

Just two more steps. My hands reached for the disk above me. Reality took on a new dimension. My leaden feet felt glued to the staples; I couldn't seem to lift them. My team members yelled encouragement: "You can do it!"

I cautiously tested the disk. My instinct urged me to kneel, then rise to a standing position. But the platform was too small. My coach called to me, "Don't kneel. You have to stand."

Fear set in. How could I stand? There was nothing to support me!

Minutes passed. My coach yelled out, "You've got to let go in order to stand."

"Let go?!" I yelled back. "You want me to *let go?!*"

I suddenly realized that this moment in time was no longer about "challenge by choice." It was something far greater: *a chance to rise above my fears.* If I could do this, then just maybe I could overcome the other obstacles in my life that were holding me back.

I thought about those obstacles: insecurity, uncertainty, the great unknown that lay in front of me after the recent death of my son, Chad. My faith had been bruised. I wanted to cry out to God, "You've given me this mountain. Now teach me how to climb it! Show me what to do!"

I looked down. My support system was in place. My team members cheered, urging me to take the next step. The chorus of encouragement rang in my ears.

But I was afraid. *Truly* afraid.

In that moment of indecision, a sudden wash of supreme peace swept over me, surrounded me, as with a loving embrace. I felt as though my son had reached out, hugged me, and said, "You know you can do it, Mom." The feeling lasted only a moment, but it was long enough.

Fearfully, awkwardly, I reached my arms out into empty space. I felt as though someone literally lifted me up. The pole swayed back and forth, and my breath caught in my throat. But in that moment I felt warmly secure. I let go and lifted my feet onto the platform—and found that I could stand!

I was as high as the treetops. I surveyed the golden colors of autumn around me, awe-struck by the beauty. My heart swelled with a wonderful sense of accomplishment. Surely God was there with me—and so was Chad.

The pole continued to wobble as I turned 180 degrees to position myself to jump. Oblivious to the echo of my team members' cheers below, I was aware only of God, my son, myself—and my choice. I reached for the sky—and jumped. Y-E-S!!

Words cannot describe my sense of elation in that too-brief time of freedom before my body was caught in the security of the belay lines and my teammates lowered me gently to the ground. I'll never forget it.

Looking back, I realize now that the climb and jump were much easier than the challenge I'd been facing every day since Chad had died. Climbing upward through my grief was much more grueling than climbing that thirty-foot pole. Some days, lifting my legs to walk forward was the biggest accomplishment of the day. Moving, just moving, no plan, no destination. Oblivious to the world, carrying out the tasks that we as survivors carry out because we have to, with very few people cheering us on.

Climbing the pole was nothing compared to what I knew now was my primary task: finding the courage to live again. My position on top of that pole paralleled the personal crisis in my life. To move forward, I needed to overcome my fears. I needed to face my predicament, make a decision, and let go of my fear. Let go of my grief.

Letting go doesn't mean forgetting; it means cherishing the memories. It doesn't mean ignoring the past; it means accepting the challenge of living in the present. Letting go is a choice that can lead to peace and purpose.

I made my choice on top of that pole. Victory over the pole! Victory over the sting of death!

A ship in harbor is safe, but that is not what ships are built for.

WILLIAM G. T. SHEDD

Tired of Hiding

Dianna Hutts Aston

I had always been a little intimidated by Cyndy, my boss's wife. She ran the business end of the newspaper he published, in addition to managing a bookstore in another town. She also served on the board of the county women's center and chaired the women's political caucus. A great-granddaughter of Czechoslovakian pioneers who settled in Texas, Cyndy had inherited their fortitude.

People took a step backward when she swept into a room on a gale of determination, capability, and strength. Her pale blue eyes softened often with laughter but then returned to their natural seriousness. There were payroll checks to write, books to keep, inventory to take, floors to sweep, dishes to wash, political fund-raisers to attend, meetings to preside over.

We were complete opposites. I was a joker. Being serious was as taxing to me as an aerobic workout. My idea of important work was lounging on the patio watching birds and clouds float by while wading in my slow-moving river of thoughts. I didn't do volunteer work—there were too many novels that needed reading. Compared to Cyndy, I was the biggest cream puff I knew, a damsel who lived on the verge of distress.

Cyndy turned out to be the white knight who rescued me.

In 1991, a year after I'd left my position as managing editor of the newspaper, Cyndy wrote an editorial called "We're Tired of Hiding." The title itself made my skin prickle, my stomach lurch. I knew about hiding. I had been hiding since I was sixteen years old.

Cyndy's editorial was a declaration of fury, her response to an alleged rapist's acquittal in another state. He was a man from a well-known family, and the facts pointed to his guilt. Across America people expected the jury to return a guilty verdict. When the acquittal was announced on the evening news, women everywhere rose up in outrage. From a rural corner in Texas, Cyndy banged out her editorial, disclosing her own rape at age seventeen.

She talked about the soul-splitting shame of it, the injustice she had discovered in the legal system, the discomfort people felt upon hearing a story of such horror. So years ago she had taken her shame and her rage, her fear and her sorrow, and squeezed it into a tiny ball that she carried around like a worry stone.

I inhaled her editorial as if it were a last breath of fresh air. Dazed, I picked up the phone and called her.

"Cyndy," I said, "I read your editorial."

"Oh, did you?" she asked casually, warily.

"That happened to me, too. When I was sixteen." I felt the wall between me and the rest of the world begin to crack. I was so tired of hiding!

She said others—women of all ages—had told her the same thing: *Me too. Me too. Me too.*

In the days after her article appeared, I thought about what Cyndy had done. She had laid open an old but still-aching wound for thousands of people to see, people who looked at Cyndy as I did, as a leader, a fixer, a doer, someone whose competence and grit was visible in the set of her jaw and squared shoulders. She had revealed a side of her that they never would have guessed existed. She had shown supreme courage: the courage to be vulnerable.

Her revelation ignited a courage in me that at twenty-seven I hadn't known I'd possessed. I began to tell the friends closest to me about my experience. It had happened in a parking lot at a shopping mall on a sunny Saturday afternoon in August 1980. When it was over and my attacker had fled, I looked in the rearview mirror of my car. I saw that I was still alive, but I didn't recognize myself anymore. It couldn't have happened to me. Not me. How could one human being violate another like that? I blinked back tears and banished the awful shame and terror to a dark dungeon in my mind. I locked it up. It was too much to bear.

Cyndy's editorial was my pass to freedom, an invitation to begin to acknowledge the blackest part of my life. The ripple effect was astounding. Half of the friends I told said, "Me too." Each one of us had borne our pain alone. Though statistics prove otherwise, we each felt like we were the only ones.

Cyndy and I took a self-defense course together after that. We learned to fight and to get away. We sweated and clenched our muscles and balled our fists and bared our teeth and annihilated our attackers, and it felt great.

Nearly ten years have passed since then. Cyndy is one of my dearest friends. We've welcomed each other's children into the world. We've weathered squalls in our marriages and celebrated anniversaries. We've walked a thousand miles around the track at the high school, talking, talking, talking. And we've held a friend's daughter in our arms as she wept her own tears of shame and sorrow. Cyndy and I will teach our daughters to fight back—and hope they never have to.

A wise woman we know once called Cyndy a "warrior." And a warrior she is. I once saw her charge a bull that had jumped the pasture fence, her only weapon a stick of lumber and a ferocious war whoop. The bull took one look at the advancing creature, possessed at the moment by the ghosts of her ancestors, her flying blond ringlets creating a Medusa effect, and leaped back into the safety of his pasture.

That's the image of Cyndy I carry in my mind: a portrait of courage.

With God all things are possible.
MATTHEW 19:26

Part Eight

RIPPLES

of

ENCOURAGEMENT

By using our hands we become strong;
by using our brains, wise;
but by using our hearts, merciful.

NICHOLAI VELIMIROVIC

His Teacher, My Hero

Dianna Hutts Aston

The postcard announcing my son's teacher for the new school year arrived in the mail a few days before school started: *Hello, James. My name is Mrs. Helm. I will be your second-grade teacher. I look forward to seeing you soon!* She had put a teddy bear sticker by her name.

Uh-oh, I thought. *Donna Helm, wife of Steve Helm, a former school-board trustee.* My husband and I had been part of a group that had opposed some of her husband's views and voted for his opponent. Now, a year later, I wondered whether Mrs. Helm would see James as the seven-year-old he was or as the son of parents who had voted against her husband.

I didn't have long to wait before learning the answer. Arriving home on the first day of school, James burst through the door, dropped his backpack on the floor and told me about his day in between mouthfuls of Lucky Charms.

"Mommy, Mrs. Helm is so nice! And Mommy, she smells like vanilla when she hugs you, and she has a son named—I forgot—and he plays football!"

I met Mrs. Helm on parents' night. With her smooth white complexion, blue eyes, and gentle voice, she was Snow White in person, and I was five years old again—small, dazzled, awed, and nervous. Her desk was in the middle of the classroom, surrounded by miniature chairs and tables, and she had placed little lamps here and there. James would spend thirty hours each week in a place that felt like home.

One afternoon a week or so after school had begun, Mrs. Helm called to chat with me about James. "First I just have to say, James is such a nice little boy. I'm so glad he's in my class." Then she told me she had observed some difficulties James was having with reading. He struggled with 'decoding,' she said—figuring out how vowels and consonants fit together to make certain sounds. She said she would work with him on it, but she wanted me to be aware of a potential problem. I wasn't alarmed, but I did feel a pang of sorrow. I knew that having a learning disability would set James apart from the majority, and learning itself would be much more difficult for him than we had imagined.

Mrs. Helm could have stopped there, alerting me to my child's problem, but then she wouldn't have been Mrs. Helm. She went on to tell me about her own experience as a young student and how she, too, had had trouble decoding. She remembered how humiliating it felt to puzzle over words and sentences that other children seemed to decipher so easily. She told me that two of her own children, now teenagers, also had weathered learning disabilities with prayers and patience and perseverance. Her youngest, Shane, was the football player James had talked about so excitedly. He had dyslexia.

Mrs. Helm not only understood how James felt, she also knew how much it hurt me to see him in tears as he tripped over word after word after word or to see his proud face fall when he gave someone a note they couldn't read. She listened quietly as I poured out my own worries and frustrations to her. Throughout first grade James had struggled with his reading homework. He whined, he cried, he yelled. He sat beside me with the book on his lap and stared at the words. It had looked to me like he wasn't trying, that he was merely resisting doing what had to be done, and it brought out the Ugly Mom in me. Was he immature? Lazy? Stubborn? I loved reading and had learned to read with ease. How could a child of mine hate to read?

The seasons of James's second-grade year drifted by. In the fall he brought home the Lucky Lefty Award, in the winter his award certified that he had the Best Sense of Humor, and in the spring he was declared the Best Helper. I appreciated the little things she did for her students. James glued those awards into his scrapbook, along with several thank-you notes she'd written to him. My favorite says, *Thank you for inviting me to your eighth birthday party. I won't be able to come because I will be watching the Aggies beat OSU. I hope you have a wonderful time. Love, Mrs. Helm.* (She did show up unexpectedly at his birthday party on her way to the game.)

During the school year Mrs. Helm and I had many conversations, usually after school when she was at home. "Modify, Mrs. Aston, you have to modify," she said. "That may mean you read a page and he reads a paragraph, or it may mean you read the whole thing to him. Just do what works for him. I remember when my son was studying for a test…"

The kernel within all her advice, though, was simply to love him and to have compassion for him. That was the tenet of her classroom as well. Under her care James bloomed and his confidence swelled. The hand on his shoulder as she checked his work, the gently admonishing glance when he should have been reading silently instead of whispering, and the vanilla hugs—James knew that she cared about him and wanted him to succeed. And he loved her for it, loves her still, with every bit of his boy's heart.

Later that year, when it was overwhelmingly evident that James had some kind of learning disability, we asked the school district to test him. The results came back on the last day of school: dyslexia. James wasn't dumb or lazy or immature. It was just that when he looked at a page of text or words on the blackboard, they jumped, jiggled, and traded places with each other, and registered in his brain in a way I still don't fully understand.

I learned over the next few months that many children aren't diagnosed with dyslexia in grade school. James was lucky. He would get the help he needed early in his education because of Mrs. Helm. Without the benefit of her experience and concern, he might have continued on to third and fourth grade, bringing home failing grades, his confidence withering, his frustration building. He might have given up.

Instead, when the next school year arrived, James was set to go. His third-grade teacher knew he had dyslexia and teaching him would be more of a challenge. He began attending daily reading and math classes taught by special educators. And Mrs. Helm was still there, just across the hall, to ask him how things were going, to smile at him, to sweep him into a sweet cloud of vanilla.

She remains only a phone call away for me too. Recently James and I made her a batch of coconut cream pudding for a Christmas gift. When I delivered it to her, she ushered me into her pink prayer room, where her angel Christmas tree stood, decorated with an assortment of heavenly creatures, glass ones and gold, feathered and frosted.

"Do you collect angels?" she asked, curious, ever gracious.

I looked into her eyes, the bluest eyes. With sudden clarity I realized the magnitude of her gifts. She had touched my son's life in a profound way, his life and the lives of hundreds of other children who had passed through her classroom. But she had also touched mine.

"No," I replied, "I don't collect angels. But sometimes I see them in people."

It is the supreme art of the teacher to awaken joy
in creative expression and knowledge.
ALBERT EINSTEIN

Brownie

Jim McClung

Camp Rainbow Connection offers a week of vacation to adults with cognitive disabilities. The activities for the week during my first year as camp director were built around the Special Olympics program. Each camper had a chance to compete in activities in which he or she felt strongest. Our goal was to help campers find an activity that they would truly enjoy.

I was anxious to meet the new campers for the week. One camper named Brownie arrived with his father, who told me his son knew all the names of Jesus' disciples as well as all the books of the Bible. I fell in love with Brownie immediately, and it wasn't due to his knowledge of the Bible. Brownie was bald like me, with a smile that could melt the coldest heart and winning ways that captivated our staff.

Many medals were awarded that first day, but Brownie won nothing. I tried to think of something that would allow him to win a medal and watched him for clues to what he enjoyed doing.

After the second day I observed that after every meal Brownie would make his way to the dandelion-covered lawn in front of the lodge. He would pick the fluffy dandelions and blow the fuzz off, giggling to himself. There was my inspiration! Quickly we added a new game to our Special Olympics roster that involved a Ping-Pong ball, a table, and blowing. I called it "The Shoot-Out at the OK Corral."

Brownie's ability to blow the Ping-Pong ball past his opponents was impressive, and he quickly defeated every challenger. Then he came up against Kathy, who had won almost everything we had played that week. Kathy stepped up to the Ping-Pong table confidently, assured that she was going to win this event, too. But after Brownie whipped the ball past her one, two, then three times, Kathy loudly declared Brownie "the best Ping-Pong blower in the whole camp!"

On the final day of camp, friends and families of the campers attended a picnic where the first-, second-, and third-place medals were to be awarded. The "medallions" were merely glorified jar lids painted gold, silver, or bronze with First-, Second-, and Third-Place written on them in magic marker, but the recipients treasured them.

One of the campers who had a generous heart and the gift of gab asked if he could give the awards out at the picnic. When he presented Brownie's award, he spoke with the eloquence of a Roman orator, waxing poetic about Brownie's accomplishment. Then, as if he were the host of *The Price Is Right,* he hollered, "Brownie, come on down!" Brownie rushed forth with more energy than I had seen in him all week. When the medal was placed around his neck, he held it in his hands for the longest time. Then, spotting his father in the audience, he held the medallion high and said happily, "See, Dad, I can do something after all!"

His response inspired thunderous applause and many tears— perhaps because Brownie taught all of us that, with a little encouragement, we can "do something after all."

Strengthen me by sympathizing with my strength,
not my weakness.

AMOS BRONSON ALCOTT

Little Brown Bear

Marjorie K. Evans

The superintendent of the school district was a gentle, kind man who considered the development of a feeling of self-worth in each child of utmost importance. He encouraged us teachers by his example to expect the children to do their very best and to motivate them with praise and loving discipline. Consequently they felt accepted and secure, enjoyed school, and achieved.

But when he retired, a new superintendent, who ruled with an iron hand, instituted different policies. This superintendent appeared to think of the children as statistics; he pressured us to push, push, push them in order to raise their test scores ever higher.

Everyone felt the tension—principals, teachers, and children— shy little Luis most of all. Finally one day he refused to do anything. He just sat at his desk looking woebegone while the other second graders worked. When I asked him what was wrong, he would just sigh, "Nothing."

At recess I talked to Luis's first-grade teacher. She said, "Let me talk to him. Perhaps I can find out what's bothering him." Finally she dragged from him, "I like my teacher…but…I don't like school much. It's not any fun."

It's about time we make it fun, I thought. So right after school I went shopping and found a delightful bear puppet made of brown felt.

The next morning I took the bear to school and placed it on my hand as I greeted my class. "Hi, girls and boys," I said, pretending my voice was the puppet's. "I'm Little Brown Bear, and I'm really happy to be in second grade. First I'm going to shake hands with each one of you. Then I'm going to sit on Mrs. Evans's desk so I can see who does nice work and is a good citizen. And tomorrow I'll sit on that person's desk all day long."

Then Little Brown Bear jumped up and down in excitement as he exclaimed, "I'm so eager I can hardly wait!"

The youngsters were enchanted, especially Luis, whose eyes sparkled. Never had I seen him work so fast or so well. Much to his delight, at the end of the day, Little Brown Bear whispered in Luis's ear that he was the best worker of the day.

The next morning Luis was at school early—tidy, clean, and with his usually tousled black hair neatly combed. He grinned with pleasure when he saw Little Brown Bear on his desk. That day he hugged the puppet, whispered to him, and showed him each work paper as he completed it.

After that, Little Brown Bear often sat on Luis's desk. Finally it was time for a parent-teacher conference with Luis's mother. He took her by the hand and proudly led her to his desk. Beaming, he handed her his work folder filled with pages of nicely completed work and with a big drawing of Little Brown Bear on the cover.

She praised Luis, then said to me, "I can't get over how much my boy enjoys school now, because he really disliked it at first."

How grateful I am that Luis reminded me that love and acceptance and expecting the very best is what motivates us—both children and adults!

Don't keep on scolding and nagging your children, making them angry and resentful. Rather, bring them up with the loving discipline the Lord himself approves, with suggestions and godly advice.

EPHESIANS 6:4 (TLB)

What Do You Want to Be?

Teri Johnson

"Mommy, what do you want to be when you grow up?" my five-year-old, Alyssa, asked. I was in the bedroom changing one of the babies, and she'd come in and plopped down beside me on the bed.

I assumed she was playing some little imaginary game, and so to play along I responded with, "Hmmm. I think I would like to be a mommy when I grow up."

"You can't be that 'cause you already are one. What do you want to be?" she insisted.

"Okay, maybe I will be a pastor when I grow up," I answered a second time.

"Mommy, no, you're already one of those!"

"I'm sorry, honey," I said, "but I don't understand what I'm supposed to say."

"Mommy, just say what you want to be when you grow up. You can be anything you want to be!"

I could not immediately respond because suddenly I was moved by her words. That tiny, five-minute experience touched a place deep within me. In my daughter's young eyes, I could *still* be anything I wanted to be! My age, my present career, my five children, my husband, my bachelor's degree, my master's degree—none of that mattered. In her young eyes I could still dream dreams and reach for the stars. In her young eyes my future was not over. In her young eyes I could still be an astronaut or a piano player or even an opera singer. In her young eyes I still had some growing to do—and a lot of "being" left in my life.

I saw the real beauty in that encounter with my daughter when I realized that in her honesty and innocence, she would have asked the very same question of her grandparents and her great-grandparent.

I once read somewhere, "The old woman I shall become will be quite different from the woman I am now. Another I is beginning..."

So...what do *you* want to be when you grow up?

Make the most of yourself, for that is all there is of you.

RALPH WALDO EMERSON

Family Resemblance

Ben Hooper

Ben Hooper, who was twice elected governor of Tennessee, told this story about his childhood. His grandson Ben Hooper III assisted with this story.

My mother wasn't married when I was born. When I started school, my classmates had a name for me, and it wasn't a very nice name. I used to go off by myself both at recess and during lunchtime because of the taunts of my playmates, which cut me deeply. Worse was going downtown on Saturday afternoon and feeling every eye burning a hole through me. Everyone wondered who my real father was.

When I was about twelve, a new preacher came to our church. I would always go in late and slip out early. But one day the preacher said the benediction so fast I got caught and had to walk out with the crowd. I could feel every eye in church on me. Just about the time I got to the door, I looked up, and the preacher was looking right at me.

"Who are you, son? Whose boy are you?"

I felt the old weight come upon me. It was like a big, black cloud. Even the preacher was putting me down, I thought.

But as the pastor looked down at me, studying my face, he began a big smile of recognition. "Wait a minute," he said, "I know who you are. I see the family resemblance. You are a son of God!"

With that he slapped me across the back and said, "Boy, you've got a great inheritance. Go and claim it."

151

That was "the most important single sentence" anyone ever said to me.

Every individual has a place to fill in the world and is important, in some respect, whether he chooses to be so or not.

NATHANIEL HAWTHORNE

A Teacher Touches the Future

Author Unknown

Teddy Stallard certainly seemed uninterested in school. With musty, wrinkled clothes, hair never combed, and a deadpan face, he exhibited an expressionless, glassy, unfocused stare. When his teacher, Miss Thompson, spoke to Teddy, he always answered in monosyllables. Unattractive, unmotivated, and distant, he was just plain hard to like.

Even though Miss Thompson said she loved everyone in her class the same, down inside she knew she wasn't being completely truthful. Whenever she marked Teddy's papers, she got a certain perverse pleasure out of putting Xs next to the wrong answers, and when she put the Fs at the top of the papers, she always did it with a flair. She should have known better—she had read Teddy's records and knew more about him than she wanted to admit. The records read:

1st Grade: *Teddy shows promise with his work and attitude, but poor home situation.*

2nd Grade: *Teddy could do better. Mother is seriously ill. He receives little help at home.*

3rd Grade: *Teddy is a good boy but too serious. He is a slow learner. His mother died this year.*

4th Grade: *Teddy is very slow, but well behaved. His father shows no interest.*

153

Christmas came, and the boys and girls in Miss Thompson's class brought her Christmas presents. They piled their presents on her desk and crowded around to watch her open them. Among the presents there was one from Teddy Stallard. She was surprised that he had brought her a gift, but he had. Teddy's gift was wrapped in brown paper and was held together with Scotch tape. On the paper were written the simple words, "For Miss Thompson from Teddy." When she opened Teddy's present, out fell a gaudy rhinestone bracelet with half the stones missing and a bottle of cheap perfume.

The other boys and girls began to giggle and smirk over Teddy's gifts, but Miss Thompson at least had enough sense to silence them by immediately putting on the bracelet and putting some of the perfume on her wrist. Holding her wrist up for the other children to smell, she said, "Doesn't it smell lovely?" And the children, taking their cues from the teacher, readily agreed with oohs and aahs.

At the end of the day, when school was over and the other children had left, Teddy lingered behind. He slowly came over to her desk and said softly, "Miss Thompson…Miss Thompson, you smell just like my mother…and her bracelet looks real pretty on you too. I'm glad you liked my presents." When Teddy left, Miss Thompson got down on her knees and asked God to forgive her.

When the children came to school the next day, they were welcomed by a new teacher. Miss Thompson had become a different person. She was no longer just a teacher; she had become an agent of God. She was now a person committed to loving her children and doing things for them that would live on after her. She helped all the children but especially the slow ones and especially Teddy Stallard. By the end of that school year, Teddy showed dramatic improvement. He had caught up with most of the students and was even ahead of some.

She didn't hear from Teddy for a long time. Then one day, she received a note that read:

Dear Miss Thompson,
I wanted you to be the first to know. I will be graduating second in my class.
Love, Teddy Stallard

Four years later, another note came:

Dear Miss Thompson,
They just told me I will be graduating first in my class. I wanted you to be the first to know. The university has not been easy, but I liked it.
Love, Teddy Stallard

And four years later:

Dear Miss Thompson,
As of today I am Theodore Stallard, M.D. How about that? I wanted you to be the first to know I am getting married next month, the 27th to be exact. I want you to come and sit where my mother would sit if she were alive. You are the only family I have now; Dad died last year.
Love, Teddy Stallard

Miss Thompson went to that wedding and sat where Teddy's mother would have sat. She deserved to sit there; she had done something for Teddy that he could never forget.

There is no lovelier way to thank God for your sight than by giving a helping hand to someone in the dark.
HELEN KELLER

Time Well Spent

Cheryl Kirking

Are you a mother? Do you ever wonder if you accomplish much each day,
When you see the floor that didn't get polished, or the laundry not put away?
If you sometimes feel discouraged, I've a few questions to ask of you—
Perhaps it's time to take a look at all the things you do.

Did you fold a paper airplane? Did you wash a sticky face?
Did you help your child pick up toys and put them in their place?
Did you pull a wagon, push a swing, or build a blanket tent?
Then, mother, let me tell you that your day was quite well spent.

Did you turn the TV off and send the children out to play?
And then watch them from the window as you prayed about their day?
When they tracked mud on your kitchen floor, did you try hard not to scold?
Did you snuggle close as prayers were said and bedtime stories told?

Did you wipe away a tear? Did you pat a little head?
Did you kiss a tender cheek as you tucked your children into bed?
Did you thank God for your blessings, for your children, heaven sent?
Then rest assured, dear mother, your time was quite well spent.

Did you make them brush their teeth today? Did you comb tangles from
*   her hair?*
Did you tell them always do what's right, though life's not always fair?
Did you quiz her on her spelling words, as you tried hard not to yawn?
Did you marvel at how tall he is, and wonder where the childhood
*   has gone?*

Did you buy another gallon of milk? Was that broccoli that you cooked?
Did you straighten your son's tie and tell him how handsome he looked?
Did you hold your tearful daughter when her teenage heart was broken?
Did you help her find some peace of mind, although few words were spoken?

Did you help her choose a college and get the applications sent?
Did you feel a little wistful at how quickly the time went?
Did you help her pack a suitcase, and try hard not to cry?
Did you tell her that you love her as you hugged her good-bye?

Do you hold them in your prayers although your arms must let them go?
Do you tell them that you love them, so that they will always know?
To make a home where love abides is a great accomplishment,
And to serve God as a mother is to live a life well spent.

Life affords no greater responsibility, no greater
privilege, than the raising of the next generation.
                                        C. EVERETT KOOP

Part Nine

RIPPLES
of
WISDOM

*The invariable mark of wisdom is
to see the miraculous in the common.*
RALPH WALDO EMERSON

A Child's Wisdom

Cheryl Kirking

A few years ago we decided to give my father a surprise birthday party. My son, who was then four, was especially excited about the party for his grandpa. Bryce spent all day making streamers, paper hats, and decorating the house. He instructed his brother and sister where they should hide and how to yell "Surprise!" with the proper inflection and zeal.

When the moment of Grandpa's long-awaited appearance finally arrived, Bryce led the troops in the noisy revelry. But as so often happens in life, reality failed to measure up to the great expectations Bryce had created. The party horns weren't tooting properly, the guests weren't appropriately enthusiastic, the cake wasn't chocolate. Finally Bryce could take no more disappointment and melted into a sobbing little heap on the floor. Scooping him up in my arms, I took him to a quiet room where he poured out his troubles to me.

"Sweetheart," I asked as he flopped across my lap, "what can we do to help you feel better?"

"Oh, Mommy," he cried between heaving sobs, "can we rewind the party?"

"Honey, I wish sometimes that we could do that, but we can't rewind time." I smoothed his golden hair from his damp forehead. "But we can start from right now and find a way to make the rest of the day better."

"Well," he sniffed, "Maybe...maybe we could just hit *pause* a little while before we go back. Okay?"

"That's a good idea," I answered, smiling to myself.

As I quietly rocked my little boy, smelling his sweet hair and feeling his warm little body relax against me, I recognized his wisdom: Sometimes, when life feels overwhelming, the best thing we can do is to just hit *pause* for a little while.

A time of quietude brings things into proportion and gives us strength.

GLADYS TABER

Let It Shine!

Cheryl Kirking

"Now it's time to go to sleep!" I said as I tried to get out of the door to my three-year-old triplets' room. I had already told three stories, listened to three very long prayers, kissed three teddy bears, a bunny, and a stuffed giraffe, gotten three glasses of water, and made three trips to the bathroom.

"But, Mommy," Bryce pleaded, "I've gotta tell you something important!"

"Go to sleep!" I replied firmly.

"But, Mommy, it's really important…you gotta come here!"

"What is it, Bryce?" I asked.

"You hafta come close!" he persisted.

"What is it, Bryce?" I repeated, kneeling beside his toddler bed. Taking my face in his soft, dimpled hands, he looked me in the eyes and whispered, "Mommy, don't ever hide your light under a biscuit!"

I assured him that I would not.

"He means basket," Sarah Jean explained from across the room. "Our Sunday-school teacher said a bushel is a kind of basket."

"Yes," offered Blake from the third little bed. "We sang about that," and he broke into an enthusiastic rendition of "This Little Light of Mine," complete with actions. "Hide it under a bushel—NO!"

"That's right, Mommy," Bryce repeated solemnly, once again cradling my face in his hands. "Don't you ever hide your light under a biscuit. You let it shine, let it shine, let it shine!"

After three more kisses, I finally made it back downstairs to enjoy a quiet moment over a cup of tea and muse over the triplets' bedtime remarks. I thought of times that I had failed to serve others because I wasn't paying attention to their needs. I recalled times that I had held back because I felt insecure about my abilities. And I prayed that God might help me and my children discover and offer our "little lights" to others, never hiding them under bushels. Or, for that matter, biscuits!

Is a lamp brought in to be put under a bushel, or under a bed, and not on a stand?... The measure you give will be the measure you get, and still more will be given you.

MARK 4:21, 24 (RSV)

A Teacher Learns
a Lesson

Cheryl Kirking

I was just twenty-two when I landed my first teaching job at a large city high school. Fresh out of college, I was anxious to teach. But I found that I still had a lot of learning to do.

I learned many things in that first year, but my greatest lesson came from John, a tall, gangly sophomore in my fifth hour American studies class. On the first day of class, John interrupted me frequently with one-liners and complained loudly about how uncomfortable the desks were for his awkward, six-foot-three-inch frame. He wasn't malicious, just pesky, but I knew I was going to have to win him over to my side or it would be a long year indeed. I could see that he not only needed a lot of attention, he was needy in other ways as well: His shoes had holes in them, and his clothes were obviously well worn.

The next day I informed John that his new seat was front row, center, where he could stretch out his long legs, under the condition that he pull his size-fourteen feet back whenever I needed to walk by.

"Admit it, Miss Kirking, you just want me closer to your desk because I'm your favorite student!" he joked.

"John, you are so smart; you saw right through my little ploy!" I joked back.

John seemed content with the arrangement, and I could tell that he tried very hard to keep his outbursts to a minimum. Whenever he was too loud or began to interrupt, an admonishing glance was all it took for him to bring his mouth under control. He was usually the first to class, which met right after lunch. He would saunter in, drop his books loudly on his desk, and announce, "Miss Kirking, your favorite student has arrived!"

"Thank you, John," I would reply with a bow, "for gracing us yet another day with your presence!"

Near the end of the first semester, I was having a particularly frustrating day. I had a terrible head cold and was grumpy and tired. The students were complaining about the upcoming final exam, and I was having trouble getting them to settle down. When I finally got everyone's attention, I warned the students, "I am passing out your assignment. I want you to get to work immediately and be quiet—and I don't want to hear one more word!"

"How about two more words?" John quipped.

"John," I snapped, "shut up!" John winced as if I had slapped him. The hurt and embarrassment in his eyes made me immediately regret my harsh words.

I was so ashamed. I had been raised not to use the words "shut up." I couldn't blame it on the unruly students or my head cold or John. I had blown it—and it was my responsibility to fix it somehow. How could I have been so disrespectful? As the sullen students worked silently on their assignments, I wondered what I should do. I feared I had broken the trust that John and I had established.

"John," I said, loudly enough for the rest of the class to hear, "I didn't show you much respect today. I am really sorry."

Still looking stunned, John shrugged and answered softly, "It's okay."

Finally the bell rang, and the class shuffled out. John lingered behind and slowly approached my desk.

"I can't believe you said that to me," he remarked incredulously.

"I know, John, I shouldn't have told you to shut up."

"No," he replied, "not that you told me to shut up. I can't believe that you said you were sorry. That's pretty cool." He gave me a little smile as he turned to leave.

John helped me learn one of my most important lessons as an educator: Respect and kindness are my most powerful tools.

> *Kindness strengthens itself by calling forth answering kindness. Hence it is the furthest reaching and most effective of all forces.*
> ALBERT SCHWEITZER

The Gift of Gab

Lynn Rogers Petrak

Although she told *me* not to talk to strangers, my mother always did. At the checkout line. Browsing through handbags at a store. During a slow elevator ride, when everyone else was seriously squinting at the buttons. At airports, football games, and the beach. I remember times when I was concerned that I had lost her in a crowd, but then I'd hear her singsong laugh and a comment like, "Yes, yes, me too."

My mother's habit of striking up conversations with strangers may bring a smile now, but it proved rather embarrassing during my tender teenage years. "Lynn's getting her first one too," she confided to a woman who was also shopping with her adolescent daughter in the bra section of our hometown department store. I contemplated running and hiding under a nearby terry-cloth bathrobe, but instead I turned crimson and hissed "Mothhhhherrrrr" between gritted teeth. I felt only slightly better when the girl's mother said, "We're trying to find one for Sarah, but they're all too big."

Not everyone responded when Mom made an observation and tried to spark a conversation. Some people gave her a tight-lipped half-smile, then turned away. A few completely ignored her. Whenever I was with her during those times, I could see that she was a little hurt, but she'd shrug the incident off and we'd continue on our way.

More often than not, however, people responded to her. Through these spontaneous chats with strangers, my mother taught me that our world is much too large—or too small (take your pick)—not to reach out to one another. She reminded me that all humans enjoy a special kind of kinship, even if we're not all that much alike on the surface. In the most mundane things, there are common threads that bind us. It may be the reason we like paper versus plastic, or why a navy sweater is never a bad buy, or why the national anthem still gives us goose bumps.

One of my last memories of my mother, when she was in the hospital and a few hours away from dying of the breast cancer that had ravaged her body, is of her smiling weakly and talking to her nurse about how best to plant tulip bulbs.

I stood silently in the doorway, wanting to cry but at the same time feeling such a surge of love and warmth. My mother taught me to see spring in others. I'll never forget it, especially now when I turn to someone and say, "Don't you just love it when..."

Kind words are benedictions.
FREDERICK SAUNDERS

Both Sides of Life

Cheryl Kirking

An ancient Greek legend tells the story of a woman who came down to the River Styx to be ferried across to the region of departed spirits. Charon, the kind ferryman, reminded her that if she wished, she could first drink the waters of Lethe, which would cause her to forget the life she was leaving.

"Oh, then I can forget all the pain I have suffered!" the woman exclaimed eagerly.

"Yes," said Charon, "but you will also forget how you have rejoiced."

The woman said, "And I will forget all my failures!"

"And also your victories," the ferryman added.

"I will forget how I have been hated," she continued.

"And," reminded Charon, "how you have been loved—and those whom you have loved."

The woman paused. In the end she decided to leave the waters of Lethe untasted, preferring to retain the memories of sorrow and failure rather than give up the memories of life's joys and loves.

To experience life fully, one must be willing to accept the pain as well as the triumph, the sorrow as well as joy. And it is the experience of the first that allows us to truly appreciate the latter.

Fortunately our minds have the wonderful ability to forget as well as remember. It is wise, then, to store the difficult memories, to keep them where they can be retrieved only as needed and not allow them to overtake our thoughts or encumber us. But the beautiful memories of love, beauty, and delight—ah, let them dance freely in our minds and hearts!

Memory tempers prosperity, consoles adversity, cautions youth, and delights old age.
SOURCE UNKNOWN

Part Ten

RIPPLES
of
LAUGHTER

There is very little success where there is little laughter.
ANDREW CARNEGIE

Mother-in-Law Misunderstanding

Gloria DePalma

My daughter's mother-in-law broke her wrist badly and moved in with them so they could take care of her while she convalesced. Helen is usually easy-going, but one evening my daughter Holly came home from work to find her in a terrible tizzy.

"Pranksters," Helen exploded. "Pranksters, that's all they are!"

Holly gently probed to find what had happened to cause this sudden personality change in her mother-in-law. And this is what she discovered:

That afternoon Helen had answered a phone call from a man who, she said, had made this statement: "Hi, I'm Jack Kevorkian. I'm coming to get rid of your pest." At a loss for words, Helen abruptly hung up the phone. *This family is trying to murder me!* she thought.

Unlike some contentious in-law relationships, Holly and Helen have always felt sincere affection for each other. So Holly did her best to assure Helen that she had no idea who the man on the other end of the phone was or what he wanted.

Nonetheless, Helen asked her son to take her home to her condo. She was quite sure her wrist had healed enough so she could manage on her own. Charlie returned a short time later minus his mother.

The next day after work Holly found the message light blinking on her phone. When she pushed the button to play the day's messages, she heard: "Hi! I'm Jack, the Orkin man. I'm coming to get rid of your pests."

A good laugh is sunshine in a house.
William Makepeace Thackeray

Too Many Ripples!

Cheryl Kirking

The other day I received in the mail a "personal" letter from a well-known female celebrity. *Dear Cheryl,* it began, *Do you know what the biggest problem is for women after age thirty?*

Hmm. The biggest problem for women after age thirty…I began to wonder. Marriage and parenting concerns? Career issues? Spiritual struggles?

Nope. According to this movie-star friend, our biggest problem is gravity. Gravity! Now, I admit I'm not fond of the ravages of gravity, but I hardly consider it my biggest problem!

Nevertheless, gravity is beginning to take its toll on my fortyish body, particularly since I gave birth to my triplets. One day while I was standing half-dressed at the bathroom mirror, getting ready to go out, my then five-year-old daughter watched intently.

"Mommy," she asked, "why is the skin on your tummy all wrinkly like that?"

"Well, honey, my tummy had to stretch a lot when I was carrying you and your brothers before you were born, so the skin never quite went all the way back."

She pondered that explanation for a moment. "Kinda like a balloon that's lost its air, huh?"

What a painfully accurate description! "Uh…yes, dear, kind of like that."

"But Mommy," she continued, pointing to my legs, "Why are your knees all wrinkly?"

I looked down at my knees. By golly, they *were* getting wrinkly.

Now I was starting to get a bit discouraged. This was one body part I didn't think had started to head south yet!

"Well, honey, that's just what happens to your skin when you get a little older," I replied.

She eyed me up and down for a few moments, her blue eyes widening, "Will your *whole body* get like that?"

"Yes," I sighed. "I suppose, eventually."

"Well," she said thoughtfully, "I guess your skin just gets tired and gives up, huh?"

> *A man without mirth is like a wagon without springs. He is jolted disagreeably by every pebble in the road.*
>
> Henry Ward Beecher

Be Careful What You Pray For!

Pamela J. Vincent

I am usually tethered to the floor by a microphone cord when I speak to groups. However, today's seminar was held in a brand new church, and the lapel mike was completely contained in my blazer pocket, allowing me freedom of movement. Just prior to stepping onto the platform in front of eighty-five women, I prayed, *Lord, help me to help them relax and grow in you.*

The purpose of my seminar is to help women better relate to their families, and participants must be willing to look at uncomfortable truths about themselves. I try to help them laugh at themselves, which I encourage by first laughing at myself to put them at ease. This day I did an exceptional job of that!

After my opening remarks, I divided the women into small discussion groups. I quietly slipped off the stage and found the rest room, knowing this would be my only chance for a break before I needed to return to the podium. As I left the rest room, I was greeted by a friend who was sitting in the back of the room. She was laughing hysterically. Reaching into my blazer pocket, she turned OFF the lapel mike! My face flushed bright red as I realized what had just happened.

"Look," my friend quipped, "at least everyone knows you wash your hands after!"

The lecture hall was noticeably silent as I approached the podium. Walking solemnly onto the stage, I took a deep bow and remarked, "Now you know more about me than you wanted to!" The place broke into applause and laughter as we resumed our tasks at hand and accomplished more than any other seminar I've done since!

You grow up the day you have your first real laugh—at yourself.

ETHEL BARRYMORE

A Rocky Vacation

Kim Allan Johnson

Deep in the remote woods of Cape Breton Island, Canada, my wife and I, with our four-year-old daughter, Stefanie, hurried to get packed and catch the fishing boat that was supposed to take us back to civilization. If rough weather prevented the boat from picking us up, we would have to hike out no later than 4:00 P.M. in order to beat the dense, moonless night.

We had trekked six miles into the wilderness the day before to trace my family roots. Gramma Hunt had grown up here over one hundred years ago. All that remained of her homestead was a rock-lined root cellar, surrounded by magnificent mountains encircling a mile-long valley that ended at the sea. I retrieved two large rocks from the cellar as valued souvenirs to present to my mom and my aunt back in the States.

We threw our backpacks onto a three-wheeled vehicle owned by hunters. Everyone hopped on, and we rode out to the beach. We waited anxiously for the fisherman to arrive as the sun arched toward the western horizon. White-capped waves kicked up by a stiff wind apparently made it too dangerous for him to come because at 3:55 the boat was nowhere in sight. I said to my family, "Looks like we're on our own. I hate to make you guys trudge all that way, but I don't see any alternative."

My wife and I donned our packs. Our little girl slipped her arms under the straps of her Mickey Mouse carryall. She usually carried a sandwich and stuffed bear inside with all the pride of a member of the Lewis and Clark expedition.

The path home was carved along the side of several steep hills that dropped away from us into the turbulent Atlantic. Even at her tender age, our daughter was a veteran climber. Stefanie had already conquered a handful of three-thousand-footers in New Hampshire. Nonetheless we noticed that she lagged behind more than usual. Several times she looked up through wilted blond hair and entreated, "Daddy, I'm really getting tired. Can we rest a little bit?" Eyeing the waning sun, I urged her on.

Two and a half hours later we exited the woods, deposited our packs in the trunk of the car, and headed off to the motel. When we stepped into the room, our daughter flopped onto the bed, exhausted. I wondered if she was coming down with a cold. As I reached inside her pack to pull out her teddy, my heart sank. Instead of feeling soft fur my fingers hit rugged stone. In my haste to leave I had placed both large cellar rocks in her little pack, thinking that we would simply dump them on the boat. By the time we started the hike, I had forgotten all about the kid-wearying load.

I didn't know whether to laugh or cry. All those miles! What a trooper she had turned out to be. I held the rocks up, tried to explain, and mumbled a sheepish apology.

Stefanie raised her head slightly from the pillow, looked at me with droopy blue eyes, and sighed wearily, "Next time, Daddy, I'll let you carry the big stuff."

I love little children, and it is not a slight thing
when they, who are fresh from God, love us.
CHARLES DICKENS

Clear As Mud

Doris Smalling and Ann Kirking Post

My husband worked hard all day trying to finish roofing our house. I tried to be helpful, taking him needed items, sparing him from climbing up and down the ladder.

"Honey," he called, "bring me the tire right away. When I finish that, I'll be done."

Eager to please, I headed for a spare tire leaning up against the garage. I did not wish to argue with him about why he needed a tire on the roof of the house.

The tire was heavy. I dragged it over to the foot of the ladder. *How am I ever going to get this heavy thing up there?* I wondered.

I shoved the end of a long rope through the center of the tire, knotted it securely, and carried the other end to the top of the ladder. I looped the rope around the rung like a pulley and carried the end back down with me. Then, feeling pride in my ingenuity, I anchored the tire in front of me on the ladder as I conquered each rung. Rung by rung, I finally reached the top just as my husband appeared at the edge of the roof.

"What on earth are you doing?!" he asked incredulously.

"You told me to bring up the tire."

His fatigue and his anger spilled over. "I did *not* tell you to bring the tire. I told you to bring the *tire*. Never mind. I'll get it myself." I scurried down, getting out of the way fast.

He hurried over to the pail sitting in the sun. I smelled the strong stench of tar as he carried the pail up the ladder. Tar? Tire? I burst out laughing. Of course! My dear husband is a southerner with a strong accent.

"What's so funny?" he asked, his irritation with me growing rapidly. "Can't you tell the difference between a pail of tire and an old tire?"

"I'll tell you later, honey." I smiled. "I just thought of something funny to put in the 'Southern Dictionary' we're making for our grand-children!"

—*Doris Smalling*

I had recently moved to Boston from the Midwest and occasionally had difficulty understanding the dialect. One day a coworker asked, "Are you going to the potty?"

A bit startled, I asked, "Excuse me?"

"Are you going to the potty?" he repeated.

I stammered for a few seconds until I realized what he meant. "Oh! The party! Yes, I'm going to the party!"

—*Ann Kirking Post*

Newspaper headlines often offer amusing reading. Here are some examples:

Two Sisters Reunited After 18 Years in Checkout Line

Iraqi Head Seeks Arms

Red Tape Holds Up Bridges

Local High School Dropouts Cut in Half

Hospitals Are Sued By 7 Foot Doctors

General Motors changed the name of the Chevy Nova after introducing the car to South America. Sales were much better after renaming the car "Caribe" for its Spanish-speaking markets. No wonder sales were low: In Spanish *"no va"* means "It won't go."

> *Words, like eyeglasses, blur everything that they do not make clear.*
>
> JOSEPH JOUBERT

Merry Mix-Ups

Various Authors

It was a seminary student in the fifties. One thing our instructors stressed was to include more modern language in our preaching, rather than using old-fashioned "religious" words.

Bob, one of my fellow students, was the guest preacher at a rural church. He was asked to give the pastoral prayer. Quoth he: "Dear Lord, please forgive us our falling shorts…"

The congregation rustled, coughed, snickered, giggled, and finally broke out in a roar of laughter. I suspect the Eternal One also grinned!

—*Rev. Robert Millner Adams*

It was obvious Pastor Young was a bit harried that Sunday morning as he jogged down the aisle with his pant leg stuck in his sock. He hurried to the pulpit to announce that the junior-high kids were going to be responsible for the entire church service this morning. He then found a pew to sit in, and one by one each child approached the podium.

The service began with the announcements. At last it was time for my son to do his part of the service. He strolled up to the podium carrying a little piece of scratch paper with Pastor Young's notes scribbled on it. He began to read:

"On Monday at 2 P.M. there will be a fun run for Myrtle Olson. She is ninety-four years old."

My husband and I looked at each other in bewilderment, not quite knowing what exactly a fun run was.

Pastor Young raised his hand, stood up, and cleared his throat. "Ah…Troy…I believe that is a *funeral* for Myrtle, not a fun run!"

—*Jorgenson Spear*

In preparation for leading music in children's church, I decided to try to get the kids more involved. The theme was God's sovereignty. I had printed very clearly on a small piece of paper, *Psalm 97:1. The Lord reigns.*

Sunday morning came, and just before we started, I asked for a volunteer to read. I chose one eager little boy in the front row. Pulling him close, I read the verse to him, instructing him to stand up and read it loudly and clearly when I asked for it. He was ready.

After singing two songs, I asked everybody to please listen carefully to the verse. The little boy rose confidently to his feet and belted out, "The Lord RESIGNS!"

What a priceless reminder that our God *hasn't* resigned, nor does he ever plan to!

—*Welby O'Brien*

Some attempts at translating from one language into another can be pretty funny if the translators don't know what they're doing. I once heard of a British missionary who was trying to translate an English hymn into a Bantu (African) language. One line of the English hymn went like this: "Sin dies, simply to rot." But the missionary's translation of the line became, "It is good for you to rot."

More recently, an American missionary in Africa attempted to translate the line: "I gave my heart to Jesus. How about you?" Unfortunately her translation gave it this meaning: "I gave my heart to Jesus. What's the matter with you?"

As a missionary to Africa with limited knowledge of Kinyarwanda, the very complicated local language, I knew better than to attempt translating. But the praise I received when attempting to speak that language was encouraging. Although a wise old African pastor translated most of the songs our school choir sang, I decided to translate just one line by myself. My little secret.

Two weeks later, the choir performed that song before a large outdoor congregation. I felt so proud hearing a big choir sing my translated line.

After the service, the old pastor respectfully approached. "Nice music," he said, "but I'm confused by that song's last line. What is it in English?"

"In English," I answered, "it's 'I believe, so why should I worry or fret?'"

Gently he explained that what I had actually translated for the choir to sing was, "I believe, so why should I throw up all the time?"

—*Carolyn Sutton*

It's a strange world of language in which skating on thin ice can get you into hot water.
FRANKLIN P. JONES

What's a Grandmother?

Author Unknown

In the words of third graders…

"A grandmother is a lady who has no children of her own. She likes other people's little girls and boys. A grandfather is a man grandmother. He goes for walks with the boys, and they talk about fishing and stuff like that."

"Grandmothers don't have to do anything except to be there. They're so old that they shouldn't play hard or run. It is enough if they drive us to the market where the pretend horse is and have lots of dimes ready. Or if they take us for walks, they should slow down past things like pretty leaves and caterpillars. They should never say 'hurry up.'"

"Usually grandmothers are fat but not too fat to tie your shoes. They wear glasses and funny underwear. They can take their teeth and gums off."

"Grandmothers don't have to be smart, only answer questions like, 'Why isn't God married?' and 'How come dogs chase cats?'"

"Grandmothers don't talk baby talk like visitors do because it is hard to understand. When they read to us they don't skip or mind if it is the same story over again."

"Everybody should try to have a grandmother, especially if they don't have a television, because they are the only grownups who have time."

A cheerful heart is good medicine.

PROVERBS 17:22

189

The Poetry
of Kid-Speak

Various Authors

In preparation for an upcoming garage sale, my little boy, Kevin, and I were sorting through our stuff. Among the treasures to sell was a toy wheelbarrow. Observantly Kevin pointed out that it was missing the wheel.

"Now it's just a 'barrow,'" he said.

—Welby O'Brien

Finally the long-awaited snow was falling, which meant school would be closed and the snowballs flying. Gazing out the living room window, my ten-year-old son and I reveled at the drifting flakes and the growing white blanket.

"Don't you just love the snow?" I exclaimed. "It's so pretty!"

"It's not the pretty-ness I like," he offered. "It's the playing-ness."

—Welby O'Brien

Having just returned from grocery shopping with Daddy, my three-year-old son regaled me with a detailed description of their shopping adventure as he happily helped me put away the groceries.

"And look, Mommy!" Bryce exclaimed, pulling items from the bag. "We bought two loaves of Kleenex and a bouquet of bananas!"

—*Cheryl Kirking*

To show a child what once delighted you, to find the child's delight added to your own—this is happiness.

J. B. PRIESTLY

Part Eleven

RIPPLES
of
GENEROSITY

Do all the good you can
By all the means you can
In all the ways you can
At all the times you can
To all the people you can
As long as ever you can.

JOHN WESLEY

Donation of Love

Cheryl Kirking

Rhonda Jensen's future seemed bright. A recent college graduate, she had moved back home with her parents to substitute teach in her hometown of Medford, Wisconsin, while she sought a full-time position. Substitute teaching can be exhausting, and since Rhonda was also the cheerleading advisor and busy with her job search, she wasn't surprised that she felt a little weary and rundown. But by November, when she still couldn't shake the cold she'd had all fall, her mother insisted she go see a doctor.

After running numerous blood tests and a bone-marrow biopsy, the doctors confirmed their suspicions: Rhonda had acute leukemia. She immediately began an aggressive course of chemotherapy. By the following September her leukemia appeared to have gone into remission, but within months she relapsed. Rhonda needed a bone-marrow transplant to save her life. No one in her family matched as a suitable donor. Doctors turned to the Red Cross national donor list.

Years earlier Elly Bertrand had seen a picture in the newspaper of a little boy who needed a bone-marrow transplant. Elly, the mother of three boys, says, "I looked at his big blue eyes and thought, 'That could be one of *my* boys. If they were ever in need, I'd hope someone would help them.'" So she registered to be a marrow donor for the little boy. She did not match. However, her registration remained on file with the national donor list.

When Elly got the call that an unidentified cancer patient needed a marrow transplant, she didn't hesitate. She didn't even know the potential recipient's name, as confidentiality is required. "I didn't even think about it." Elly relates. "I was excited!" Medical experts cautioned, however, that there was only a 25 percent chance that Elly would match the anonymous recipient.

She matched.

And so Rhonda Jensen received Elly's bone marrow. The transplant procedure went well, although the recovery process was slow. After one year, during a medical checkup, Rhonda was finally given the name of her donor. She was surprised to discover the donor lived in a nearby town. "I didn't meet Elly right away. I just didn't know how to go about thanking her for saving my life." So Rhonda wrote to Elly, and their friendship grew through the exchange of many letters and pictures.

Rhonda continued to thrive. She and her high-school sweetheart, Kevin, set a date to marry. Their wedding had been postponed due to Rhonda's health problems, but she was now much stronger.

Unbeknownst to Rhonda, her sister invited Elly to the wedding shower and hid her in a back room until Rhonda arrived. The first meeting between Rhonda and Elly was an emotional one for all present. That June, Elly was an honored guest at the wedding, where the pastor publicly thanked her for making the marriage celebration possible. Elly's generosity had touched the lives of everyone present that day.

But within a year Rhonda again faced desperate trouble. Her kidneys had been severely damaged by the strong medication and radiation used to treat her leukemia and were operating at only 10 percent of normal function. Rhonda's only options were lifelong dialysis or a kidney transplant. Once again, no one in her family was a suitable donor. Then the transplant specialist recommended they contact Elly. Since Rhonda had received Elly's marrow, their kidneys would match like those of biological twins.

Rhonda couldn't imagine asking Elly for such a sacrifice. "There was no way I could see myself asking her for another life-saving part," Rhonda recalls. Unlike marrow, a kidney could not be replaced. "I didn't want to ask her. How do you ask someone who has given so much to give even more?" After three months, though, she decided to send a letter to Elly. Rhonda felt that by sending a letter she could give Elly the chance to digest the idea. "For my own piece of mind, I had to ask, to at least give her the chance to consider it," Rhonda explains.

What did Elly think when she received the letter? "It scared me at first. I thought, 'What if my boys should ever need a kidney?' But no one in Rhonda's family was a match. A complete stranger matched better than anyone in her family. Then I thought, 'That could happen in my family too.' If it did, I would sure hope that someone would be willing to help."

Elly's husband and boys told her they would support her in whatever decision she made. But other family members were not so sure. Hadn't she done enough?

What would Elly's decision be? Elly gave Rhonda a clue on the fifth anniversary of the bone-marrow transplant, an important milestone for marrow recipients. Elly sent Rhonda a bouquet of silk lilacs. Attached was a card, asking for her to pray for Elly's family to support her decision.

Elly soon went to the University of Wisconsin Hospital in Madison for testing, to make sure she could withstand the surgery. When it was confirmed that she could, she immediately telephoned Rhonda.

"What are you doing May 5th?" Elly asked.

"I don't know for sure," Rhonda answered.

"Well," replied Elly, "you could get a kidney transplant."

The transplant went smoothly. Rhonda's fatigue was immediately gone. Elly's kidney matched so well that Rhonda wouldn't even need the anti-rejection drugs that could increase her chance of relapsing into leukemia again. It was the first time in history that a nonrelative had made both a marrow and an organ donation to the same recipient.

Elly's gift of life continues to have a ripple effect in the lives of others, far beyond Rhonda and her family. The amazing story has received national coverage on the NBC *Dateline* television program, resulting in many viewers signing their organ donation cards. Untold lives have and will continue to be touched by Elly's selfless sacrifice.

Elly remains humble about her donations. "I think God had it all planned out, long before our time."

Says Rhonda, "I think Elly's an angel sent down from God—an angel that hides her wings."

Only love can be divided endlessly and still not diminish.

ANNE MORROW LINDBERGH

Problem or Solution?

Edgar Bledsoe

It was 1933. I had been laid off from my part-time job and could no longer make my contribution to the family larder. Our only income was what our mother could make as a dressmaker.

Then Mother was sick for a few weeks and unable to work. The electric company came out and cut off the power when we couldn't pay the bill. The gas company cut off the gas, and except for the intervention of the health department, our water would have been cut off as well. The cupboards got very bare. Fortunately we had a vegetable garden and were able to cook some of its produce over a campfire in the backyard.

One day in the midst of all this, my younger sister came tripping home from school with, "We're supposed to bring something to school tomorrow to give to the poor."

Mother started to blurt out, "I don't know of anyone any poorer than we are," but our grandmother, who was living with us at the time, shushed her with a hand on her arm and a frown.

"Eva," she said, "if you give that child the idea that she is 'poor folks' at her age, she will be 'poor folks' for the rest of her life. There is one jar of that homemade jelly left. She can take that."

Grandmother found some tissue paper and a little bit of pink ribbon with which she wrapped our last jar of jelly, and Sis tripped off to school the next day proudly carrying her "gift to the poor."

It was a good lesson for all of us: learning to see ourselves as part of the solution even when we, as members of the community, were involved in the problem. My sister never thought of herself as "poor folks," and ever after, whenever there was a community-wide problem, she made herself part of the solution.

A bit of fragrance clings to the hand that gives flowers.

CHINESE PROVERB

Blossoms of Kindness

Betty Kehl

I remember last spring watching the first shoots of grass lifting their heads and testing the air. The grass didn't seem to grow fast enough after the long Wisconsin winter.

To nurture my longing for spring, I visited the local garden center, all the time dreaming about summer: birds chirping, warm breezes, cats pouncing on imaginary bugs before reclining beside the flower bed as I worked.

Finally it seemed safe enough to purchase the plants without putting them through a late frost. Pansies were my choice; their hooded faces seemed always smiling as they danced in God's creation. Having a very small garden, I had to choose every plant painstakingly. Sunny yellow and purple, a calm peach, majestic white and purple, velvet purple with specks of yellow.

As I was paying for the plants, the cashier commented on the stately beauty of a gigantic white-and-purple pansy. It did seem to stand out over all of the rest, and I nodded with pride, mentally planting it in the center of my garden with all of the other flowers around it, paying homage.

After I returned home, just as I was about to begin tenderly transplanting the pansies, my eight-year-old neighbor, Kim, came over to investigate. Her eyes lit up when she saw the flowers. Kim's family doesn't plant a garden, so the year before I had given her a pansy to plant next to her house. This seemed like a good tradition to keep up, so I asked her if she was ready to pick a pansy. She smiled, knelt down, and longingly touched the petals of several plants.

Somehow I recognized myself in this eight-year-old. I held my breath, though, as she constantly came back to my prized white-and-purple pansy. The other flowers were so colorful—surely the white pansy would be safe! But no, that white pansy with the smiling purple face commanded attention. Kim's blue eyes were sparkling as she picked up the "white king" and sprinted to her house with her new prize.

As I adjusted my mental picture of my garden—without the giant pansy at its center—I felt a sense of loss. A flower is such a small thing, but that pansy was a difficult one to give up. I knew it was right, however, to give, and I remembered that God wants us to give of our "first fruits." I decided that rather than feel bad, I would rejoice that I could give such a remarkable flower to a little friend.

And all summer God blessed me for my hesitant gift. Kim and her dad planted the pansy by the corner of their house. There it prospered, and I saw it every time I drove into my driveway. I smiled every time I passed it.

But God wasn't finished blessing me yet. I had planted some bushes the summer before, highlighting them with a one-time planting of pansies. I had planted no seeds or seedlings around them this year, yet pansy after pansy, with no help from me, pushed through the earth and blossomed. Every time I admired God's garden, I thought of Ecclesiastes 11:1: "Give generously, for your gifts will return to you later" (TLB).

And still God was not finished with his blessings. Recently, after several frosts, I stepped outside into an unusually warm day for a Wisconsin November. Walking around the grounds, I noticed empty birds' nests in bare trees and leaves spinning over the ground. When I came to my garden, everything was brown and frozen and dead...except for one giant, perfectly formed pansy growing in the middle of my garden! I knelt to examine it. The purple-and-white petals were so soft to the touch...

Kindness is the sunshine in which virtue grows.
ROBERT G. INGERSOLL

The Ripple Effect

Carl Cunningham

As the editor of a newspaper, I see a lot of mail tumble across my desk. Most of it is junk mail that ends up in the garbage. But one letter stood out from the others that day, just a few days before Christmas. The pretty handwriting attracted my attention. In the letter Michelle Stegall, of Groves, Texas, shared with me how a stranger's kindness had touched her life and the lives of many others.

One December Michelle was picking up some odds and ends at a local store. Her basket contained a variety of common items—shampoo, wrapping paper, dog food, and a few small Christmas presents. The clerk had already begun ringing up her items when Michelle realized she had no cash with her and she had just used her last check.

She nervously asked the clerk to "hold my stuff," as she put it, so she could quickly drive home and get more checks. She tore out of the store, red-faced and annoyed with herself. When she returned to the store ten minutes later—to the same checkout lane—she found that her items, about fifteen dollars' worth, were gone.

"They put it all away, didn't they?" Michelle asked the clerk. But no—the clerk handed her a bag containing all her items. "I started to pay," Michelle wrote, "but the clerk told me it was all paid for. She explained, 'The lady that was behind you in line earlier said to tell you "Merry Christmas,"' she said. My mouth just fell open. A total stranger had paid for my things!"

Michelle's mystery woman didn't leave her name with the clerk, and no one else seemed to know anything about her, but whoever and wherever she is, Michelle wants her to know how much her kind and generous gesture meant to her. "When I was in line,"

Michelle remembered, "she was worried and kept asking me how much more money I needed and made sure that the clerk was really going to hold my things for me. We chatted a little about the holiday season, and I apologized for holding up the line. She was very understanding."

Of course everybody else in line wanted to know the story, and Michelle told them. "I just want to tell her thank you," Michelle said, "and that I truly appreciate what she did for me. She's received many prayers out there because of it. It's kind of like a ripple effect."

In fact, the "ripple effect" Michelle spoke of began at a Christmas tree farm near Groves that was sponsoring a fund-raiser for Zola Fleneken. Zola had taught school in the area for forty-two years and was in need of money for a liver transplant to save her life. The check Michelle had written for a tree was the last check in her checkbook and the reason she didn't have cash when she got to the checkout stand.

"It cost a bit more than the other trees," says Michelle, "but it was for a good cause. I thought in the back of my mind that my caring would come back to me someday."

Little did she know it would come back to her just minutes later! The kindness and generosity of the woman who paid her bill made Michelle ponder the meaning of giving and the spirit of Christmas. "Maybe letting as many people know what she did is my way to thank her," she says. "Her kindness has touched so many more lives than just mine. It really has had a ripple effect."

Little acts of kindness are stowed away in the heart like bags of lavender in a drawer to sweeten every object around them.

SOURCE UNKNOWN

Just Because

Sharon Dalton Williams

I had been at work all day and had just spent an hour driving through rush-hour traffic. All I wanted to do was sit down, eat supper, and relax. But when I arrived home, my husband met me at the door. The cats were out of food, he told me, and we would have to go to the store.

Very reluctantly I changed my clothes, grabbed the grocery list, got back into the car I had left just moments before, and drove with my husband to the grocery store.

The store was packed. I groaned—this wasn't going to be a quick trip. My husband grabbed a grocery cart, and we navigated our way through the store aisles in search of the items on our short list.

Because the store was so crowded, maneuvering through the aisles was difficult. I got more and more irritated as people rolled their carts in my way or stopped in the middle of the aisle to look at something, oblivious to the fact that they were in the way. Children were crying or pulling items off the shelves. The longer we stayed in the store, the shorter my temper got. I had just about had enough.

Meanwhile my husband serenely followed me through the jungle of legs and wheels. At one point I managed to squeeze through a blockade, but my husband had to wait a moment until the blockade moved before he could progress ahead with the cart. After he broke free, another shopper pulled right in front of him to reach for something on the shelf, causing him to wait yet again. I watched in amazement as he smiled at the person and backed up a little to allow her better access to the items.

When the person had moved on, I asked my husband whether or not the people around us were bothering him. He said, "Not really." I asked him in an irritated tone why he allowed people to get in his way and slow him down when we were in a hurry to get out of the store. He calmly replied, "Because I want to be nice to people."

Sometimes generosity can be as small a thing as being nice to people under trying circumstances. My husband had quietly reminded me of what was really important in life, and suddenly the grocery store seemed a little brighter.

Stop complaining about the management of the universe. Look around for a place to sow a few seeds of happiness.

HENRY VAN DYKE

Part Twelve

RIPPLES
of
DELIGHT

*I am beginning to learn that it is the sweet, simple things of life
which are the real ones after all.*
LAURA INGALLS WILDER

Grass

John W. Doll

My mother had experienced many of life's tragedies and few of the compensations. She lost our dad after only a few years of marriage and was left with two young boys to raise during the Depression of 1929. She gave up her job as a trained nurse and governess to a millionaire's children to do housekeeping in order to keep the remains of her family together. Although her hands looked like a construction worker's from scrubbing clothes and floors, God was kind and gave her ninety-three years with minimal sickness. She never had much time to sit down and teach me about life, but I gained a world of knowledge in values and living by watching how she treated and talked to people.

After getting my brother and me through school, her greatest joys were a TV I had bought her, an occasional visit from my brother, who lived farther away, and Sunday mornings when I would take her to breakfast.

It was one of these mornings, following a week in which my life seemed a study in futility, that I learned a valuable lesson from my mother. At the time, the only beauty in my world was knowing I had at least twenty more hours before I had to start a new workweek.

It was a cool, California summer morning. As I drove up to my mom's old house, she was already sitting on the rough front porch. Mom loved her little old house, the first permanent residence she had ever enjoyed. As I got out of the car and walked toward the porch, I could see that her tired old face was radiant with love and the anticipation of the short ride to the neighborhood coffee shop and breakfast.

Her black shoes were immaculately polished as usual—as neat and clean as her black skirt and simple white blouse. The blouse was pinned closely around her neck with a blue swallow brooch that had the word *Mother* spelled out in gold wire on it. I remembered having given that cheap little pin to her on a Mother's Day at least forty years earlier.

I helped Mom into the car, and as we drove off, she said—as she did each Sunday—"My, my, Buddy, what a beautiful car." I'd bought it new two years before, but I looked at it as old. Twelve more months of payments and I could get a new one.

I sincerely wanted to make Mom feel that the next few hours we spent together were as important to me as I knew they were to her, but I was distracted, too totally convinced of the ugliness of the world to enjoy myself. Each time she spoke, it was of joy and hope, and each time I heard myself replying with a courteous answer but without genuine interest or encouragement. We finished our breakfast, and I drove her back home, another Sunday visit coming to an end.

I was looking at the street, in need of patching, and the houses, badly in need of paint, when suddenly, as if she were seeing a sunrise for the first time, Mom exclaimed, "Oh, Buddy, look, look! Isn't it beautiful?" It was about 11 A.M.—there certainly wasn't any sunrise. What could be so beautiful on this dingy old neighborhood street? Again, as a courtesy, I responded, "What, Mom? What is so beautiful?"

"The grass, Buddy, the grass. Look how beautiful the grass is!" At first I thought, *Beautiful grass?* As I turned to look at the grass, I saw Mom's wrinkled old face, her thinning white hair, and her long hands, the enlarged veins and knuckles earned from eons of sacrifice and love. Her old, dimming eyes were bright and shining, and her face was radiant with a smile as she pointed to lawn after lawn of plain green grass.

I have seen beautiful faces for quite a few years now—but none as beautiful as this old lady as she rejoiced in the beauty of ordinary grass. How rich and endowed she was to find and see the beauty in the ordinary! How impoverished and unfortunate I was with my shallow sense of values! As my eyes left her face, I looked at the grass in shame. Like a miracle, I thought I could hear beautiful music. But even more miraculous—the grass *was* beautiful!

I returned my gaze to my mother's face, so lovely as she looked at me, as if to say, *See, Buddy? You can see it too. The grass is beautiful.*

I didn't want to say a word. I was afraid the magic would pass, that I would lose this wonderful, warm peace.

I helped her from the car and opened the front door of my mother's home. "Well," she said, "thanks, Buddy, for this beautiful morning. I know you're very busy. What are you going to do with the rest of your day?"

I hoped my guilt wasn't showing and that she could feel my gratitude for the lesson I had just learned. I took her in my arms and held her tightly as I whispered in her ear, "Mom, I'm going to rush right home and look at the grass."

"Det som ar omtyckt ar altid vacker": That which is loved is always beautiful.
NORWEGIAN PROVERB

Nice Words

Cheryl Kirking

My triplets, age three, were playing nicely together, so I took advantage of the moment to rest for a few minutes. I grabbed a pillow and lay down in the hallway at the top of the stairs. From this spot I could hear everything that was going on in the family room below without being seen or, I hoped, interrupted.

After about three minutes I could hear Bryce saying to the others in his sweet lisp, "Come on, Sarah Jean! Come on, Blake! Let's clean up the toys for Mommy!" His words were followed by the sound of toys being tossed into the toy chest.

But Bryce's siblings weren't helping. "Come on," he urged. "Then Mommy will say, 'Oh, what a nice surprise!'"

Again I could hear toys being tossed into the toy box, but obviously only Bryce was doing the work.

"Okay, but if you don't help, you won't get any of Mommy's nice words!"

Oh, my heart completely melted! "Mommy's nice words!" I realized just how important our words of appreciation are. When we tell others we are grateful for their efforts, it inspires them to continue to do good works.

Thank you—such "nice words."

> *He that receives a gift with gratitude repays the first installment on his debt.*
>
> SENECA

An Attitude of Gratitude

Cheryl Kirking

One morning I poured my first cup of coffee and opened the morning paper to the daily advice column. This letter warmed my heart.

> Dear Ann:
>
> How I wish I were a really good writer. Then, maybe I could put my thoughts into words and let you know exactly how I feel. I am an 86-year-old woman who is still keeping house, driving my car, and enjoying life. I was blessed with a wonderful husband. He lived to celebrate 61 years of marriage with me.
>
> This morning, I decided to do some washing. I put my clothes in the machine, patted the side of the washer, and said, "Do your job." And it did! While waiting for my washing to be done, I sat in my living room and watched TV—waiting for the "ding" to tell me the washing was done. Then, I got up and put the clothes in the dryer.
>
> Sitting there, I thought: Dear God, what a wonderful life I lead. How blessed we are with all the modern conveniences. Do we appreciate them? Then, I looked in my kitchen and saw an electric stove, a microwave, a refrigerator, a toaster, a mixer, and many more items that I haven't listed.
>
> I am not wealthy, but I'm not poor, either. I am just a simple, average, middle-class old lady who is living on Social Security and feeling truly blessed that I live in this wonderful country of ours.
>
> (signed) Mary Tury in California

I loved this simple letter of gratitude! I decided to track Mary Tury down, and after a bit of sleuthing, dialed her number. A sweet voice answered the phone. "Hello?"

"Hello, my name is Cheryl Kirking. Is this the Mary Tury who wrote a letter to Ann Landers?"

"Well, yes it is!" She laughed.

"I just wanted to tell you how much I enjoyed your letter," I explained. "What prompted you to write it?"

"Well, just like I wrote—one morning I put my wash in and patted my washer like I always do and said, 'Do your job!' And it did. I was just feeling thankful, and I thought to myself, I'm going to write to Ann Landers. So I did. I was so surprised when one morning I saw my letter in the paper, though. I never dreamed it would be printed!"

"Have you gotten much reaction from it?" I asked.

"Oh, heavens, yes. I live in a mobile park, and when I went to play cards that day, all my friends said, 'Well, here comes the celebrity!' I've gotten phone calls from all over the country. One woman in Alaska called and talked for forty-five minutes. She was so depressed and said she wanted to feel the way I do. She had money and all the things it buys, but I guess she needed to be reminded to be thankful for the everyday things."

I guess we all need to be reminded of that from time to time. Thank you, Mary.

Gratitude is a vaccine, an antitoxin, and an antiseptic.

JOHN HENRY JOWETT

A Big Surprise

Norma B. Larson

"Guess what's in my hand?" I challenged the five-year-old students in my Sunday-school class. I thought I was offering them a surprise, but I was in for a big surprise myself.

Most of my students' guesses involved treats or food of some sort—wishful thinking. I gave a few clues, but no one guessed. Finally they decided to give up.

As I unclenched my fist, they shrieked. From a minute hole in the acorn I held, a tiny green worm poked its head out. The timing was absolutely perfect.

"Do it again!" they commanded.

As if I could. It was a once-in-a-lifetime show stopper. And one little fellow summed it all up when he pronounced, "God did it."

*Nature is the face of God. He appears to us
through it and we can read his thoughts in it.*
                                          VICTOR HUGO

A Real Vacation

Cheryl Kirking

"Mama, when can we take a vacation?" I whined.

"Why, honey," Mama seemed genuinely surprised. "We just had a vacation!"

"When?"

"Just now! We just took the whole afternoon off to relax—we had a nice drive and bought ice cream! That was a vacation!"

"No, I mean a *real* vacation. Like Debbie's family. They just got back from Mackinac Island in Michigan! Last summer they went to the Wisconsin Dells. We never go *anywhere*."

My mother never put up with whining, and this time was no exception. She didn't say a word, just gave me her "You know better than that" look. It was very effective—kind of a sad look, with a trace of disappointment in her soft brown eyes. I knew I had crossed the line when Mama gave me that look. I sighed loudly as I flopped down on the cool green grass to mope. But I knew better than to say any more.

We had just returned from a family drive. Nine of us had piled into the '62 Ford station wagon—five kids, my parents, Grandpa and Grandma. Being the youngest, I started the trip out on my usual seat—the hump over the transmission. But predictably, my stomach turned with each twist in the country roads, so I'd moved over to Grandma's lap by the window.

I strained to breathe some fresh air. The window was opened only a crack, since the gravel roads kicked up a lot of dust. By the end of the trip I'd been passed forward to sit on Grandpa's knee in the front passenger seat. "Watch the road, Cheryl Lou, then you won't feel so carsick," Grandma suggested. It didn't work.

"Hank's corn looks good," my father commented.

"Sure does. But look how last week's downpour washed Charlie's field." Grandpa shook his head at the erosion. "Lost a lot of good topsoil." The owners of the fields we passed had once been Grandpa's neighbors, before Daddy and Mama took over the family farm.

My dad began to whistle "Mockingbird Hill," as he always did on those drives, keeping the beat by tapping his wedding band on the hard metal steering wheel.

As much as I loved my family, those occasional Sunday drives were certainly no vacation. To me they were torture. Breathing "used air," as I called it, feeling queasy from motion sickness, my sweaty legs sticking to the seats. True, it was a rare treat to buy ice cream cones at the country store, but I remember mine melting so fast in the heat that I hardly got to eat any of it. My oldest brother kept licking my cone.

"Mama! Make him stop!" I squawked.

"I'm just helping her," my brother explained, all logic. "It's dripping all over." I was lucky to get half of it.

Today, some thirty years later, I'm reclining on the same patch of grass where I lay pouting after that Sunday drive. The grass is cool on my bare legs, just as it was then. The soil smells musty, and the breeze lulls me to a lazy state of serenity. I remember that day vividly, along with countless other memories that tumble around in my heart and head...

Feeding the sheep that grazed beyond the white wooden fence, the fence I'd climb to pick cherries off the tree.

Helping hang laundry on the clothesline, the damp clothes smelling fresh of homemade lye soap.

Playing hide-and-seek on warm summer nights.

And I remember chasing lightning bugs, the hem of my nightgown, damp with dew, tangling around my ankles. And my brother, the same one who ate my ice cream cone, patiently helping me fill my empty peanut butter jar with the twinkling fireflies. Sometimes my mother would let me take them to my bedroom. We put plenty of holes in the jar lid, and I'd always let them fly free in the morning.

I remember gathering eggs with my sister in the chicken house up the hill and helping Daddy on his weekly egg route to Madison.

I'd stack the empty cartons from the previous week while he wrote up the bill to the restaurant and store owners who counted on him to keep them supplied with fresh eggs. We also delivered our eggs to homes, even though it probably wasn't worth the time or the gas; most of our customers were getting on in years and, with their kids grown and gone, bought only a dozen or two. But my dad didn't have the heart to cut them out of his route, and he always took an extra minute to ask about their health and families, even though it meant he'd be later with chores and milking that night. I could tell the customers looked forward to my handsome, likable father's visits, and I always felt proud of him.

Once a year, in the early spring when the buttercups and Dutchman's breeches were in blossom, Mama would pack a picnic lunch and we'd all trek down to the grove of trees beyond the pasture. It was just a ten-minute walk, but it seemed like a long, adventurous hike back then. Mama was always in the lead, the five of us kids tramping behind like ducklings in a row.

My recollections carry me back to a time of security and stability. I am overwhelmed with gratitude. Grateful that my own children can pick cherries as I had, chase kitty cats in the barn, help my mother in the big garden. Thankful that my little girl has shared giggles and secrets with my niece in the big brass bed upstairs, just as my sister and I did so many years ago. Grateful my children can spend time in this place where honesty, integrity, and hard work aren't just quaint ideals but a way of life modeled by their grandparents.

"Whatcha doin', Mom?" I squint up at my six-year-old son, his blond hair shining like spun gold in the sunlight.

"Oh, just listening," I answer.

He settles down beside me, arms behind his head. "I don't hear anything."

"Keep listening," I tell him. "You will."

We lay quietly, side by side, looking up through the white branches of the birch tree, the spring green leaves dancing against an azure sky.

"Ah...," Blake sighs. "This is the life, huh, Mom?"

"It sure is," I murmur. "A real vacation."

Big doesn't mean better. Sunflowers aren't better than violets.

EDNA FERBER

If I Could Hold This Moment

Cheryl Kirking

Little one, so soft, close your sleepy eyes,
Breath of an angel, gentle baby sighs.
Go to sleep my love, and I will sing a lullaby—
If you wake or if you cry,
I'll be here.

If I could hold this moment and keep it for my own...
Surely this precious moment is the sweetest that I've known!
The softness of your tiny hand, the warm scent of your hair—
I delight in your babyhood, but I can't keep you there
For other voices call, and you've so much more to grow;
So I'll learn to gather memories, as I learn to let you go...

Little one, you've grown so strong and good and bold
Off to find adventure, discoveries untold!
Run and play, my love—here's a kiss to take along.
I'll watch from the window,
I'll be here.

If I could hold this moment and keep it for my own...
Surely this precious moment is the sweetest that I've known!
To hear your laughter as you play, see the sunlight in your hair—
I delight in your childhood, but I can't keep you there,

For other voices call, and you've so much more to grow;
So I'll learn to gather memories
As I learn to let you go...

God gave his children memory
That in life's garden there might be
June roses in December.

G. A. STUDDERT-KENNEDY

Contributors

Robert Millner Adams has been a pastor in Wisconsin for fifty years. A native of the New Jersey coast, he graduated from Western Maryland College near Baltimore and Garrett Seminary at Northwestern University. His motto: "A sense of humor is God's grace working."

Dianna Hutts Aston has worked as a journalist and editor and has a degree in journalism from the University of Houston. She writes from her home in Central Texas, where she lives with her husband, David; her children, James and Elizabeth; and old dog, Bear.

Glenda Barbre developed a love for writing while still a child in the small town of Rhododendron, Oregon. As God's plan unfolded in her life, she began writing stories of blessings. She teaches writing workshops and shares her Native American heritage by teaching others how to make root baskets.

Edgar Bledsoe, born on a farm in northeastern Missouri, was one of the "Okies" who went to California in the 1930s when the Depression interrupted his studies at Texas Tech. After a successful sales career with Kaiser Aluminum Co., he retired to live in Green Valley, Arizona, with his wife, Marian.

Renee Bondi, a gifted Christian singer, has a dynamic speaking ability that grabs her audiences, which range from large Christian conferences to women's events. For booking information contact her at www.reneebondi.com or Capo Recording, P.O. Box 459, San Juan Capistrano, CA 92693.

M. C. Burns is an editorial writer for the Syracuse *Post-Standard* and the *Herald American*. She started her journalism career in Belfast, Northern Ireland, and worked stories in Kenya, Haiti, Ireland, and the Philippines. She received a Robert F. Kennedy Journalism Award for her coverage of the famine in Somalia. She has also been honored with state and local journalism awards. She is married and has one son.

Annie Chapman is a popular women's conference speaker, singer, and author of numerous books, including *Gifts Your Kids Can't Break, Smart Women Keep It Simple, What Do I Want?* and *Running on Empty.* Married to Steve Chapman and mother to Nathan and Heidi, she encourages women with her humor, songs, and keen insight.

B. J. Connor and her husband, Michael, have a daughter, Nichole, and a son, Sean. B. J. met Doris Delventhal at a Bible study at their church in Ann Arbor, Michigan. A former newspaper writer, B. J. has been published in twelve books and numerous magazines, including *Guideposts* and *Focus on the Family.* She is a 1999 Amy Writing Award winner.

Carl Cunningham is the managing editor of the *Mid County Chronicle* newspaper. Married with two little girls, he is also a freelance music writer and has interviewed, photographed, or reviewed stars including Little Richard, Willie Nelson, Neil Young, Chuck Berry, and Bo Diddley. A Seattle music collector, he runs Internet consignment auctions in his spare time.

Doris Delventhal, a Michigan native, is a retired registered nurse busy with family and volunteer work. After graduating from nursing school, she moved to Denver, Colorado. There she met Leo, a graphic-arts professor. Their children, Mari Lee, Fred, and Barb, their spouses, and six grandchildren help make Doris's life beautiful.

Gloria DePalma holds a bachelor's degree in education and is secretary to the director of trust services for the Northern New England Conference of Seventh-Day Adventists. She has taught for twenty years in parochial and public schools. She enjoys writing and has had several articles published. She and her husband, John, have four adult children.

John W. Doll began writing lyrics in Chicago for Lawrence Welk. He continued writing after moving to California. He is a regular contributor to the very successful *Chicken Soup for the Soul* series. He lives on an orange grove with his wife, Lanie. John recently completed a book titled *Autumn Leaves Around the World.* To order, contact him at 2377 Grand Ave., Fillmore, CA 93015 or fax (805) 524-3821.

Wendy Dunham is a wife, a mom, an author, and a therapist for differently abled children. After dishes are done, homework's complete, laundry's sorted, and her children asleep, Wendy can be found writing. Contact: 3148 Lake Rd., Brockport, NY 14420.

Colleen Edwards is a part-time inspirational writer and a full-time marketing executive in Orange County, California. Her next goal is to spread the message of love and hope to children through writing and speaking engagements. Editorial/publisher inquiries welcome. Contact: 26566 Calle Lorenzo, San Juan Capistrano, CA 92675.

Marjorie K. Evans, a former elementary-school teacher, is a freelance writer who has published a number of articles. She and her husband, Edgar, enjoy grandparenting, church, reading, gardening, raising orchids, and their Welsh corgi. 4162 Fireside Circle, Irvine, CA 92604-2216.

Victor Fried combines storytelling with poetry, demonstrating inspirational truths that have moved audiences nationwide. If you are interested in having Victor come speak to your church or civic organization, write: The Dreamweaver Project, 9 Music Square South, Ste. 181, Nashville, TN 37203, or call (615)327-0031

Vivian Gall is described by friends as "Born reading and writing." After twenty-five years of teaching, her idea of retirement is working as the school librarian at the same school where she taught. Two daughters and two granddaughters keep her world full of wonderful stories.

Teresa Griggs bears a true testimony of comfort and strength through the storms of life. She actively shares God's message of hope with a warm smile and encouraging word as she speaks to women across the country. E-mail: Griggs@bootheel.net.

Beverly Harding-Mullins is author of the book *Called to Be His Servant: H. C. Kiser Jr.* Her story in this book, "Liberation Day," is an adapted excerpt from that book. After pursuing a career in social work, Beverly is now a full-time mother and homemaker. She lives in Abingdon, Virginia, with her husband, Mike, and children, Christy, Kyle, and Rachel.

Wayne Holmes of Fairfield, Ohio, is a husband, father, and freelance writer as well as a creative storyteller and, as you'll learn from his story, "The Fall of Humpty Dumpty," an enthusiastic juggler!

Roy Wayne Howard is a country music artist from Dupo, Illinois. He wrote his first song at ten years old and has been playing guitar and singing for forty-five years. He has been compared to Johnny Cash throughout his career. You can hear selections from his latest CD at www.MP3.com/bigroy.

Liz Hoyt is a freelance writer in the Texas hill country. Besides raising a teenage grandson, she is a busy volunteer and illuminates life through her stories of the heart. Contact her at 106 Seamoor, Fredericksburg, TX 78624, or mehoyt@fbg.net

Kim Allan Johnson lives in Pownal, Maine, with his wife, Ann, and is the associate treasurer of the Northern New England Conference of Seventh-Day Adventists. He has authored two books, *Spiritual Body Building* and *The Gift,* and written articles for various magazines. Kim preaches and conducts seminars from Toronto to Florida.

Teri Johnson currently co-pastors the First United Methodist Church of Brookings, South Dakota. She loves preaching, writing, and teaching. Teri and her husband, Marty, are the parents of five children: Taylor, Alyssa, Alec, Emily, and Elliot. She can be reached at 625 5th St., Brookings, SD 57006.

Laura (Gorka) Kaiser is a much-loved wife and the mother of a teenage daughter and places a very high value on "being there" for her family. She enjoys reading, counted cross-stitch, and playing the piano as well as a full schedule doing volunteer work with her family.

Kurt Kaiser has more than two hundred copyrighted songs to his name. He has arranged and produced albums for many gifted artists, among them Larnelle Harris, Burl Ives, Christopher Parkening, George Beverly Shea, and Joni Eareckson Tada. His piano album *Psalms, Hymns, and Spiritual Songs* received a Dove Award. In 1992 he was awarded a special Lifetime Achievement Award from the American Society of Composers, Authors, and Publishers.

Betty Kehl is a "wordsmith" who practices her craft in many ways, including teaching high-school English in Waterloo, Wisconsin. She is published in ten different poetry anthologies, having won first place in a national contest.

Cheryl Kirking is the Ripplemaker™ who compiled this book. She is a songwriter, author, and popular conference speaker. For more information, see "About the Author" at the end of this book. For booking information or to order her CDs and tapes, contact P.O. Box 525, Lake Mills, WI 53551. Web site: www.cherylkirking.com.

H. C. Kiser Jr. now 76, resides in Abingdon, Virginia, with his wife, Grace. They have two children, Cindy Howard of Harlan, Kentucky, and Mike Kiser of Chattanooga, Tennessee, and three grandsons, Kyle Howard, Evan Howard, and Austin Kiser. To purchase a copy of *Called to Be His Servant,* please send $8.95 plus $2.00 shipping and handling to: Called to Be His Servant, P.O. Box 1091, Damascus, VA 24236.

Norma B. Larson is a retired teacher, feature columnist, former sorority magazine editor, and author of a sorority history. She describes herself as a "wanna-be journalist" and considers her finest accomplishments marrying her college sweetheart, rearing her three fine sons, and becoming a mother-in-law and grandmother.

Carmen Leal is the author of *Faces of Huntington's* and the coauthor of *Pinches of Salt, Prisms of Light*. She is also the author of *WriterSpeaker.com*, an Internet guide for writers and speakers. For more information or to contact Carmen, visit her Web site: www.writerspeaker.com.

Florence Littauer is a dynamic speaker who has inspired audiences worldwide. She is the best-selling author of numerous books, including *Personality Plus, Put Power in Your Personality!* and *Silver Boxes*. For information on seminars and workshops, please call (800)433-6633 or see the CLASS Web site: www.classervices.com.

Marita Littauer is a professional speaker with over twenty years' experience. She is the author of nine books, including *Personality Puzzle, Come As You Are,* and her newest, *You've Got What It Takes*. Marita is the president of CLASServices Inc., an organization that provides resources, training, and promotion for speakers and authors. Marita and her husband, Chuck Noon, have been married for seventeen years. For more information: www.maritalittauer.com.

Jim McClung is a United Methodist pastor in Richmond, Virginia. He is the founder of Camp Rainbow Connections, a camp for mentally disabled adults. A writer and songwriter, he is currently working on a book of his experiences.

Roberta L. Messner, Ph.D., is a registered nurse, quality-management specialist, speaker, and author of over a thousand stories and articles and several books. Her medical, inspirational, and home-decorating articles have appeared in more than one hundred publications. She is a regular contributor to *Guideposts,* and her work has appeared in *Chicken Soup for the Soul* books.

Dennis Myers is a husband, father of four, and grandfather of three and lives in a suburb of Kansas City, Missouri. His passion is writing inspirational stories, fiction, and nonfiction. He is also the editor of a monthly genealogical publication.

Welby O'Brien is author of the book *Formerly a Wife* (Christian Publications). A conference speaker for ministry leaders, women, and singles, she is also featured in the video *Fulfillment for the Single Heart* (Western Seminary Productions). She and her son live in Portland, Oregon.

Malcolm Patton is pastor of Gallatin First United Methodist Church in Gallatin, Tennessee. He has been serving churches since 1957. He and his wife, Barbara, have two sons, Christopher and Timothy, and a grandson, Blake. He is a Lions Club member and on the board of directors at Cumberland Mental Health.

Rochelle M. Pennington is a newspaper columnist and has contributed to *Chicken Soup for the Soul*, *Life's Little Instruction Books*, *Stories for the Heart*, and *The Proverbs 31 Ministry*. She coauthored *Highlighted with Yellow* with the best-selling author H. Jackson Brown. You may contact her at N3535 Corpus Christi Cir., Campbellsport, WI 53010, or call (920) 533-5880.

Lynn Rogers Petrak is a freelance writer who lives in LaGrange, Illinois with her husband, Michael, and two children. She has written for the Chicago *Tribune, Chicago Magazine,* and *Romantic Home Magazine,* among other publications. Her submission is written in memory of her mother and great friend, Carol Rogers, who died in 1994 after a courageous nine-year fight with breast cancer.

Ellen Seibert Poole freelances as a writer and vocalist/musician in Portland, Oregon. This wife, mother, and occupational therapist on "creative sabbatical" has published short pieces for book collections and articles and publicity materials for churches and professional and community organizations.

Ann Kirking Post, a mother of two, has traveled extensively around the country in her role as program manager for National Outreach at the Smithsonian Institution. She has encountered many regional dialects and colloquialisms but is usually able to make herself understood!

Kaye D. Proctor is a social worker living in southern Oregon. For many years she worked as a therapist in mental health and alcohol/drug rehabilitation. Writing is one of her passions, along with parenting her beautiful twin daughters.

James Robison is an evangelist whose ministry, LIFE Outreach International, works in twenty countries around the world, particularly where the physical needs are staggering. James and his wife, Betty, host the syndicated television program *LIFE Today.* He is the author of more than a dozen books, including *My Father's Face* and *Knowing God As Father.* Contact LIFE Outreach International at P.O. Box 982000, Fort Worth, TX 76182-8000.

Fred M. Rogers is the well-known creator and host of the television program *Mister Rogers' Neighborhood.* Also an ordained Presbyterian minister, he has inspired children and adults alike through his television program and writing.

Kathleen Ruckman has been married to Tom, a physician, for twenty-six years, and resides in Eugene, Oregon. Mother of four, Kathleen is a freelance writer of magazine articles and short stories and teaches women's inductive Bible studies.

William Schlegl is the author of nine religious puzzle books. He has had hundreds of religious puzzles published in over twenty-one different denominational magazines. Bill and his wife, Eleanor, live in Quincy, Illinois.

Doris Smalling, published author and poet (Valley Forge National Poetry Award), enjoys her husband, three grown children, five grandchildren, teaching, and public speaking. Contact: 1137 N. Harrison CT, East Wenatchee, WA 98802, or e-mail at dpsmalling@aol.com.

Jorgenson Spear packs a pen and pad wherever she goes. Her desire is to capture pieces of life, pour them out onto paper, and bless those who will listen. She is married, with three sons, a daughter, a daughter-in-law, and three grandchildren. Contact 2596 50th St., Granada, MN 56039.

Gloria Cassity Stargel is an author, a freelance writer, and an assignment writer for *Guideposts* magazine. She shares her own spiritual journey as she witnessed a miracle in *The Healing: One Family's Victorious Struggle with Cancer*, available for $9.95 plus $3.00 postage and handling by calling (800)888-9529 or visiting her Web site at www.brightmorning.com.

Tom Suriano is the son of Jim and Evelyn Suriano of Martins Ferry, Ohio. He and his wife, Kim, have two daughters, Susan and Stephanie. Tom holds a master's degree in counseling and has twenty years' experience in education. He is a high-school guidance counselor and football coach.

Carolyn Sutton is a former teacher, missionary, and editor and currently is a rancher's wife and freelance writer and speaker in Oregon. Carolyn has written *Journey to Joy, Eye-Openers, Fool's Gold,* and *No More Broken Places,* as well as numerous articles and stories.

Jeannie St. John Taylor is the author of several children's books. She lives with her husband, Ray, in Portland, Oregon, on a farm surrounded by subdivisions. Her three children attend college nearby. She is also an artist and a private investigator.

Mary Tury never thought of herself as a writer, but her letter to Ann Landers touched the hearts of millions. Mary, eighty-seven, has celebrated sixty-one years of marriage to her husband and has three children. She enjoys playing cards with her friends and is grateful to live in this wonderful country.

Pamela J. Vincent started her writing career as an academic educator in the home-schooling market. Her book *Gate-Keepers at Home* helps women discover their protective roles as the hub of the family. A speaker, she encourages parents to be all they can be. E-mail: TRECer (503) 637-3162.

Jeannie S. Williams is a writer, speaker, and magician and has entertained audiences for years with her special blend of creativity and humor. She is author of the children's book *What Time Is Recess?* and is a frequent contributor to the *Chicken Soup for the Soul* and *Stories for the Heart* book series. She is founder of Unlock the Magic creative writing workshops. For information, write P.O. Box 1476, Sikeston, MO 63801.

Sharon Dalton Williams lives in Laurel, Maryland, and has published articles in Christian magazines and published submissions in a yearly women's devotional book. She also writes and publishes a monthly devotional tool entitled *Word in Due Season.*

Nancy Zastrow is a writer and editor of *Wings,* the newsletter of a nonprofit organization that helps those coping with grief. To contact Nancy or to subscribe to the *Wings* publication: P.O. Box 1051, Wausau, WI 54402-1051. Tel: (715) 845-3424.

Permissions and Acknowledgments

A diligent search was made to identify original ownership of the pieces in this collection. For permission to reprint any of these stories, please contact the original source (see "Contributors" section for contact information.)

Grateful acknowledgment is made to the following for permission to use their material. Acknowledgments are listed by story title in the order in which they appear in the book. Stories of unknown origin and those in public domain are not included in this listing.

About the Author

Cheryl Kirking tickles the funny bones and tugs at the heartstrings of audiences nationwide by weaving homespun humor and common sense with her touching stories and original songs. Through her Ripples Unlimited™ Keynotes, concerts, and workshops, she encourages others to identify, develop, and use their talents. She seeks to base her life and work on 1 Peter 4:10. "As each has received a gift, employ it for one another, as good stewards of God's varied grace" (RSV).

Cheryl has given hundreds of presentations for associations, hospitals, businesses, government agencies, school districts, parenting groups, and churches since she began speaking professionally in 1989. She draws upon her professional background in high-school teaching, lay ministry, and public relations to enhance her presentations. She is an alumnus of the University of Wisconsin–Madison and a member of the National Speakers Association.

She is a contributing author to numerous books, including the best-selling *Chicken Soup for the Soul* series. She has recorded six CDs of original songs on the Mill Pond Music label—but she considers her nine-year-old triplets her greatest production!

Her greatest joy is being mama to Bryce, Sarah Jean, and Blake. They keep her days slightly chaotic and her heart delightfully full. She shares life with them and her husband, David Kilker, in a house by a woods.

To contact Cheryl, please write to:
Ripples Unlimited™
P.O. Box 525
Lake Mills, WI 53551
Or visit her Web site at www.cherylkirking.com

More Splashes, More Ripples!

If you have a heartwarming, humorous, or uplifting story to submit for consideration for future volumes, please write to:
   Ripples Unlimited™
   P.O. Box 525
   Lake Mills, WI 53551

Or submit your story through Cheryl's Web site:
   www.cherylkirking.com.